Grumpy Middle Aged Dad and Lottie - More Adventures In Orlando

Grumpy Middle-Aged Dad and Lottie – More Adventures In Orlando

From the Author:-

I have tried to recreate events, locales and conversations from my memories of them. In order to maintain their anonymity in some instances I have changed the names of individuals and places, I may have changed some identifying characteristics and details such as physical properties, occupations and places of residence. Any names or characters, businesses or places, events or incidents, are fictitious. Any resemblance to actual persons, living or dead, or actual events is purely coincidental.

All proceeds from this book were donated to the Meningitis Now charity. I did not make a single penny from this book – if you have reason to be offended, please don't sue me.

Michael Hadley

The Black Country, November 2018

For Charlotte Moon Hadley.

Now and forever, my Star Girl.

I love you,

Dad x

5 star Amazon reviews for The Grumpy Middle-Aged Dad – Adventures in Orlando

Facebook- @grumpymiddleageddadblog

"What a fabulous book! I had tears rolling down my face from start to finish. One of the funniest things I have ever read! Do yourself a favour and pick up a copy – you won't be disappointed!" – L M Kimberley

"One of the funniest books I've ever read and I can relate to nearly everything in it." – Peter Harper

"Absolutely loved this book! Was a great read and definately loads of lol moments!!" – Melissa Folkes

"Hilariously accurate… especially holidaying with teenagers. I cried with laughter. This is a man who adores his family. I can't wait for the next book." – Kay Steven

"Dad, you're not even funny." – Lottie

"Read this whilst on the train to London. People were looking at this crazy woman who was laughing out loud and just couldn't stop. That was me. A lovely funny read." –Vonnydee

"Loved it!! It was so funny from start to end!! Read in one day as I couldn't put it down." – kimmy

"Woof!" – Molly the Cockapoo

"I bought this as a present for my Dad for Father's Day as we have been to Orlando many times and my dad would sometimes be a bit grumpy! After giving it to him, he read it within two days and was in stitches especially as he found it so relatable. Now the whole family want to read it." – KPollak

"Great book. Laugh out loud funny for anyone who has trudged the paving stones around Disneyworld. This book reminded me so much of our family trips and I think we can all be Mr / Mrs Grumpy sometimes. Well worth a read." – Lindsay

"Absolutely excellent read, totally relatable, proper laugh out loud funny" – Amanda Mansfield-Clark

"Funniest book I've read in ages!! I enjoyed it so much read it in one sitting" – pf watson

"Can you hurry up and finish this sodding book as you're getting on my nerves now" – Wifey

"Highly entertaining read!! Definitely the book to leave in the bathroom for ALL to enjoy. Combination of Disney magic and grumpy British humour = Fantastic". – Jade

"Can I borrow some money dad?" – Sam

"I followed with interest the Grumpy Middle-Aged Dad's adventures around Orlando in his blogs, so when these were turned into a book I just had to read it. The book is both heart-warming and laugh-out-funny and clearly written with much love. Michael Hadley is a very funny man and a gifted writer" – Amanda Graham

"Read the blogs daily and they were hilarious – bought the book and had a sore face from laughing so much!! If you have ever been to Disney world or even if you haven't this is the funniest best description of the place!! 5 stars Mr Hadley, a fantastic read!!" – GLB

"I have just finished reading the antics of Grumpy & want to ask when's the next book out? I feel like I've been on the holiday with The Fam & experienced all that they have. I happen to know Grumpy & can say how proud I am of him & this truly hilarious read, in fact I wish they'd stayed for longer just so I could read more! The level of description easily transports you there (alongside Grumpy in the laundry room) for that I LOL. I got some looks at work, chuckling away to myself...so what if I should have actually been working!
So Grump, pull ya finger out ar kid & get writing the next one!" – A Black Country Lass

"Love love love! So funny, anyone who's been to Orlando can relate to Grumpy's musings. Lighthearted and fun, and raising money for 2 great causes. Highly recommended!" - Jacqui L.

"A must read for all Disney and Orlando fans everywhere. This will make you laugh out loud. For those of you who think Disney is a waste of money and 'not for you' then you too will enjoy the tongue in cheek reviews!" – Helen Ellis

Grumpy Middle Aged-dad (and Lottie) – More adventures in Orlando

Contents

Acknowledgements

The success of my first book, *Grumpy Middle-Aged Dad – Adventures in Orlando*, led to a life changing 12 months for me. I've met some amazing people and made some great friends. I also received a huge amount of support before, during and after from some truly wonderful people that I'm lucky to have in my life.

More importantly, it also resulted in thousands of pounds raised for charity which in turn would have been put to great use by The Neuro Foundation and Follow Your Dreams.

If you bought my first book, and you are now obviously in possession of my second one, I cannot thank you enough. Your support means so much to me and I thank you from the bottom of my heart. If, on the other hand, you have not read the first book I urge you dear reader to give it go as it's way funnier than this one.

It is my absolute honour and privilege to give special Grumpy mentions to the following wonderful people who went above and beyond in helping to make this book a reality.

Peter Harper, Paul Elwell and Tony Fullam from *Orlando Info Zone* and *It's Orlando Time* - two amazing Facebook sites packed with great info and lovely people and where I posted all the original blogs. An extra nod to the *Orlando Info Zone* admin team too, who are simply a wonderful group of people who I am proud to know – your collective loveliness reflects on me and makes me seem a much better person than I really am.

The team from Meningitis Now, my chosen charity who will receive the proceeds from the sale of this book. If you read right to the end of the book, you will know why this is so important to me.

Ruth Cleeton, my super mum-in-law and proof reader extraordinaire who corrected my gramma and helped to construct it in to a book n that, and Tara Hooper who also helped dotting t's and crossing eyes.

Thanks to my mum and dad for... urmmm... basically everything. I'm eternally grateful for your love, help and support and you're both at the beating heart of everything I've ever done and achieved. Oh, and especially for introducing me to the music of Barry Manilow as a teenager. Not forgetting my little sister Josie who helped with my social media and stopped me from getting beat up by the big boys at Dudley Comprehensive.

To Wifey Catherine and Handsome Boy Sam, thanks for putting up with my bad moods, bad jokes and being Grumpy all the time. Oh, and for letting me and my little girl go off to Orlando without you both. Ya day miss much...

Finally, to my beautiful daughter and travelling companion, Charlotte Moon Hadley – I love you with every beat of my heart and I am amazed that a bozo like me helped to create such a wonderful, loving, caring, special human being.

Whatever you do and wherever you go, you will always be my little girl.

Sir Grumpalot of the Black Country - A Short Fairy-tale

Once upon a time in a land far, far away, just off junction 10 of the M6, there lived a chubby but nevertheless ruggedly handsome knight who went by the name of **Sir Grumpalot of the Black Country**.

Sir Grumpalot resided in a small semi-detached castle in Deepest Dudley, where he grumpily spent his days as a miserable Managing Director of a car parts mining company. He was married to the kind and beautiful Lady Grumpalot, and in between trips to IKEA, quarrelling and one of them having the hump they had somehow managed to raise two fair skinned Teenage Children - Handsome Little Lord Grumpalot and Pouty Princess Lottie Grumpalot. They were joined in the semi-detached castle by a delightful animal by the name of Molly the Cockapoo who was surely the cutest, shaggiest haired mutt in all the kingdom.

Throughout the long days flogging his guts out in Deepest Dudley, Sir Grumpalot dreamed of a Magical Land on the other side of the vast ocean. A Magical Land full of delightful laughter, captivating wonder and adrenaline fuelled excitement. A Magical Land full of temptation for the heart and belly where you can Magically blow your life savings in only a matter of a few hot, bad tempered days.

A Magical Land called **Orlando**.

One day, after a particularly hard and frustrating shift down in the car parts mine in Deepest Dudley, Sir Grumpalot returned home in need of a shot in the arm. He needed a fix of Orlando videos so whilst waiting for Lady Grumpalot to provide the evening vittels, he withdrew to the parlour, sparked up the mystical Microsoft Surface Pro Looking Glass and logged on to Ye Olde You Tube.

After an eternity waiting for Ye Olde Sky Broadband to work, Sir Grumpalot watched said videos in awe and wonder as joyful families made lifelong memories, kids screamed happily with excitement and Grumpy dads sold kidneys to pay for it all.

Imbibed by several large glasses of ancient mead (Bombay Sapphire and Fevertree Tonic) Sir Grumpalot lifted his handsome head from the Looking Glass, and through blurry, bloodshot eyes, he looked deep into the night sky above the scratchings factory and had a vision.

A vision of **HIM** in that Magical Land!

A vision of **HIM** shrieking with laughter!

*A vision of **HIM** experiencing unending joy, making lifelong memories and shaking off the troubles and woes of working in Deepest Dudley.*

*A vision of **HIM** realising he's totally skint as his credit card crashed through its limit and promptly melted.*

Gaining mystical power and Dutch Courage from the Bombay Sapphire, Sir Grumpalot rose majestically from the parlour table, and letting out a triumphant roar and a boozy hiccup, he professed:

"A QUEST! Forsooth, this IS MY destiny... I must travel to this Magical place and see for myself the wonders of Orlando!"

Sir Grumpalot recruited Princess Lottie to join him on the Quest as despite being really strong and brave, he didn't fancy going on his own as it's a bit weird. The beautiful and kind Lady Grumpalot was excepted from the Quest as she had lots of very busy things to do like look after the semi-detached castle, play Ye Olde Candy Crush and throw balls for Molly the Cockapoo. As for Handsome Little Lord Grumpalot, he wished to remain at home with his loyal band of merry men, chasing fair maidens in Ye Olde Discos of Dudley. Dilly dilly.

Shortly after, there followed a live chat with a fair young damsel from the court of Sir Richard of Branson and in only a matter of moments Sir Grumpalot had magically spunked 6 months' salary for two uncomfortable seats on a cramped flying machine and bedding in a small room at Ye Olde Hard Rock Inn.

Just at that moment, the beautiful and kind Lady Grumpalot walked in from the scullery with tea and noticed the browser page still open on the mystical Looking Glass and therefore spotted the price of said quest.

Thus ensued the almightiest of rows as tempers flared, crockery smashed and Sir Grumpalot coming close to becoming a divorced eunuch.

Undeterred, brave Sir Grumpalot was destined for the Magical Land, and so with heart full of enthusiasm and promised plans to Lady Grumpalot that he will help round the house a bit more and do lots of car boot sales to raise the extra coffers, he started on Ye Olde Magical Countdown.

Read on, dear friends, for more tales of Sir Grumpalot and his trusty sidekick Princess Lottie, as they embark on more adventures in the Magical Land that is Orlando.

Ye End

The Brain Fart Strikes Again

I reckon that Brain Farts should be recognised by the medical profession as a serious illness, especially in middle-aged men. When you get to my age, I know it's important that you watch your cholesterol, cut down on fatty foods and do more exercise, along with every so often asking someone to stick their finger up your bum to check your prostrate *, but I think there should also be compulsory Male Brain Fart Screening.

(* Be careful when / who you ask. This is the main reason I'm banned from Asda in Dudley).

As soon as they hit 40, all men should be sent a letter from the local health authority calling them in to be asked a set of simple questions about their current mental state and daily activity. Questions such as:

Have you ever been sent out for milk and come back with a bag full of groceries but no milk?

Have you ever reached for the remote control to turn the volume down at the pictures?

Have you ever strode purposefully in to a room to suddenly realise that you have no idea why you're there?

Have you ever been sent out for milk and come back with a new conservatory?

Since your 40th birthday, have you given in to the urge to buy a pair of red trousers?

Have you ever impulsively purchased any keep fit contraption off the teleshopping channel (for example, an Abs Trainer, a mini trampoline or a Bullworker), only for it to be left under the sofa that you slouch on every night?

Have you ever been sent out for milk and gone back home drunk 4 hours later?

If the answers to any of these questions are yes, then the man should be immediately sedated by being locked in a room and shown a slideshow of Holly Willoughby photos. When he's nice and dopey and dribbling on his shirt, executive powers, car keys, PIN numbers and credit cards should be taken off him and handed over to his next of kin.

I'm a prime candidate for Male Brain Fart Screening. I have Brain Farts on a regular, almost daily basis, ranging from minor ones like pouring tea on my cornflakes to bigger, life threatening ones like turning myself in to a human Guy Fawkes whilst trying to light a bonfire with petrol.

Both true, by the way.

In fact, as I've got older and more stupid, a lot of my Brain Farts have taken a more dangerous twist as I've found new ways to attempt to accidentally kill or maim myself. Such as:

> Skiing right over the edge of a cliff when I thought I knew where I was going.
> Tipping a mini digger over on myself showing off and just about escaping through an open window.
> Being chased through a field of cows and having to hide by climbing up a tree.
> Somehow scalding my gonads whilst trying to steam my sinuses.

All the above are true. The last one is my favourite

My latest Brain Fart, however, was of the financial sort and led to booking another expensive trip to Orlando.

In early June 2018, just before my daughters 18th birthday, in a desperate moment of gin-fuelled weakness laced with a few dollops of melancholy (more of that later) I lost all semblance of monetary will power.

There is no excuse, I know, but in my defence the situation wasn't helped by the fact that I was both bored and a bit tipsy whilst browsing the internet. This is always a lethal combination, akin to putting a chimp in charge of a tank or electing Donald Trump as President.

Always interested in finding out new things, I had very innocently Googled "Virgin in Wolverhampton" and after spending a couple of hours or so being totally shocked by what I saw and having to delete my browser history, I eventually landed on the Virgin Atlantic site.

As I looked dreamily at holidays I could never afford, a little box popped up on my screen and a I was asked if I wanted a "Live Chat". Not having learnt my lesson from the last time this happened to me which ended up with a £96.58 bill to Babestation, I proceeded to engage in a very nice "Live Chat" with an *actual* Virgin girl.

She was absolutely lovely and in my mind's eye actually looked and sounded like Holly Willoughby. Things were going great for a short while for me and virtual Holly – she seemed genuinely interested in me and we chatted about things we had in common, places we'd been, holidays, you know that sort of thing. Just as I was about to ask her "What's Philip Schofield **really** like?" she upped the ante by saying she knew exactly what I needed and that she could get it for me… right now.

I admit I may have totally misread the situation and her keenness to talk to me. Like most blokes with no back bone, the sight of a pretty female face or a quick flash of a bra strap is enough to make me melt like butter in the sun, making it almost impossible to say no to anything (this is why in the last few years we have had two extensions on the house, a new bathroom, a new kitchen and Molly the Cockapoo, despite the fact I'm allergic to dogs. I'm well and truly wrapped around Wifey's alluring bra strap)

Holly's seductive words and alluring promises of personal adventure made me putty in her virtual hands. The temperature rose as the chat blossomed and by now Holly and I were both all in on a flirty conversation that was building up to a mind blowing, leg shaking, duvet gripping crescendo… and, just as it did with Babestation, ended abruptly as soon I'd handed over my credit card details.

Quicker than you can say "please don't tell my wife" I'd swapped 365 days' worth of disposable income for 2 flights on one of Richard Branson's shiny red planes and 8 days in a hotel room jointly owned by Mr Hard Rock and Mr Universal.

Still, the damage had been done and as I sobered up in the coming days and came to terms with my rush of blood, I realised that there was at least one consolation. Barclaycard were really, really happy with me. In fact, they must have identified me personally as someone they'd like to do more business with as they wrote a very special letter offering to lend me even more money should I need it – you know, if I ever got in a pickle, like.

How kind! They know I'm good for the money as I've still got one kidney left.

My sole travelling companion this time is my beautiful teenage daughter Lottie. This is for a number of reasons I'll explain later but mainly because Wifey decided to stay at home as she's in training for when Candy Crush is officially named as a new discipline at the next Olympics, and Handsome Teenage Son is busy being chisel jawed and cool whilst learning to be a pilot.

Oh, another reason why Wifey won't come with us is because she daren't leave her precious Molly the Cockapoo with a dog sitter. Molly got dead mad with us the last time we went away and it took ages to get over the trauma of staying with the neighbour for three weeks. God knows what went on next door, but when she got back she had a glazed, distant look, matted fur, sported a red bandana and had learnt to say in a croaky voice:

"You weren't there, man... you weren't there"

How strange.

After last year's adventure in Orlando with The Fam and the incredible year I've had since as a result, the desire to go back and do it all again was really strong. The holiday in itself was truly wonderful, despite my literary grumblings, and not only did we make lifelong memories, but it also enabled me to fulfil my ambition to write the first book.

So, in a rather pathetic attempt to justify the cost of the above Brain Fart, it seemed sorta right to me to fly back again to experience a little more Orlando magic and record my experiences along the way for this, the second book.

And if I was scrambling around looking to find another reason to justify the Brain Fart, I've got a spanking good one. This time around it's just me and Lottie, and I love my little girl to bits. I want to squeeze out every drop of Daddy / Daughter time before it's too late.

The plan is to spend 8 full on days ripping up Universal, hopping over to Disney Hollywood Studios and Magic Kingdom, being chased by alligators on an airboat ride and a day at Seaworld whilst having laughs, making memories and writing down funny stuff in between.

And loads and loads of time spent with my wonderful, zany, bonkers Teenage Daughter Lottie before she realises that it's really not cool to go on holiday with just your dad.

A little about Lottie

At this point in the book I better do something that I was taught in the half day *"How To Write Your First Novel"* class I attended at Dudley Leisure Centre.

If you have had the benefit of reading my first book, you will almost certainly know that I completely and utterly winged it – I'm still amazed that Mr Amazon decided to publish it at all to be honest. I'm still expecting to get a belated e-mail from one of his Chief Executives at some point saying:

"Woah, woah, woah… what's all this shit about?"

Worried that someone from Amazon might actually read this nonsense before they print it next time, I decided to get some "professional" help with this new one to make it look dead good n that. Oh, and also just in case some literary agent stumbles across my drunken ramblings and decides to give me a 6 book deal with a ten grand advance like that woman who writes those "Why Mummy Drinks / Swears / Snorts Coke" stuff.

Ever the cheapskate, I truly believed that for just £30.00 (including light refreshments) some failed local English teacher with bad breath, a scruffy beard and acute dandruff could actually teach me how to construct, edit and publish a book after just four hours study in a musty room above the squash courts.

I'm pretty sure that's not how J K Rowley started.

To no-one's surprise, the class was utterly useless. The first half an hour (or £7.50) was spent going over the fire drills, health and safety and Dudley Council's LGBGT equality policy and the next 30 minutes talking about the new Black Country By-Pass.

Then as soon as the bearded blunder launched into his introduction about the craft of writing, two blokes in front of me got up and left as they incorrectly thought they were on the speed awareness course.

The only bit of good information that I learned from that miserable 4 hours is that if you want to become a literary genius like me, you have to introduce the characters early on in the book so you, the reader, has some idea who I'm talking about and what on earth is going on.

So, settle down as I'm going to tell you about my beautiful little girl Lottie, and why the two of us are going on holiday together.

Lottie, or Charlotte Moon Hadley to use her full name, had just turned 18 a few weeks before we left for a little adventure to Orlando. The mini holiday was, amongst many other things, part birthday present / part reward for working so hard at her A levels - which I'm happy to say she passed with flying colours and will soon be off studying to be a paramedic.

As I write this, she's got two part time jobs to earn some extra cash for more online shopping and she's learning to drive in a 10 year old Micra christened Marge. She also has a boyfriend called Sam who is a great lad and really looks after her. (So far, he's passed the Dad test, but sssshhh... don't tell him I said so, ok?).

She is a wonderful daughter, a fantastic sister to her big brother (also called Sam) and an all-round beautiful, fabulous human being. When we are at family parties or social get togethers, Lottie always looks great – she's polite, courteous, funny and engages in conversation with anyone. She has a maturity well above her years and is loved by all the family.

In an age when there's so much pressure on young girls to always look like they're at a nightclub or they feel it's ok to share semi naked, pouty pictures with the world, Lottie just does her own thing. These pictures disturb me – the only time I would have seen anything like that as I was growing up would have made the middle pages of Razzle.

She dresses how *she* wants, doesn't bow to peer pressure and has developed a strong character with a deep sense of independence. I don't think it would be possible for me to be any more proud to say she's my daughter and I love her with all of my heart.

All of the above is fab – there can be no greater reward as a parent than to see your child blossom and grow in to a whole, grounded human being fit to take on the big old ugly world and all the idiots that's in it.

Well, before Donald Trump has blown us all up, that is.

Except for one thing - the fact that she's growing too quickly in to a beautiful young woman and is no longer *my* little girl.

I wouldn't change a thing of course, but god almighty I miss the days when Lottie and her brother Sam were little.

There are many moments that you remember as a parent – that precious first smile, the unforgettable first word and those first few wobbly steps.

And of course the later landmarks as they grow from little toddlers to kids, like the first day at nursery school, losing their first tooth or having their first crush. Then the transition from Primary School to "Big" school, and that first picture in their ill-fitting uniform (you know, the one's we all *love* on Facebook and the one we're going to use on their 21st birthday party invite)

Oh, and there's the Prom thing of course. That's another, relatively new rite of passage and something that Grumpy Dads struggle to get their frazzled, miserable heads round.

Sorry, I'm going to go off on a rant here as I just don't get it.

You would think given the amount of money spent on age-inappropriate sparkly dresses, mega tons of hair lacquer and gallons of foundation and mascara that these kids had a <u>real</u> cause for celebration.

Something *really* good, like collectively finding a cure for cancer by accident in chemistry, winning the Nobel Peace Prize for an essay in English Lit. or cracking the code to find the secret of why X Factor is <u>**still**</u> on my telly.

But no, the reason why these teenage girls "dress" like they're off to a gypsy wedding with uncomfortable hair and eyebrows that look like they've been put on with a bingo dobber is simply that they've just left school.

That's it. That's all it is. **They've just left school.**

Thousands of pounds wasted on dresses, hair, make up and pink limousines just to spend a few hours pretending to be drunk on Aldi orange squash in the Premier Inn function room on a retail park in Dudley.

I must have missed the memo on this as when I left school in the Black Country we never had a prom, or even a leaving disco. Well, not that anyone told me about. When I left school, I got egg and floured, had my shirt ripped to shreds and my shoes lassoed over the phone line with their laces tied together.

And to this day I'm still not convinced that all the other dads did it to their kids.

Anyway, these and many more are little markers in their young life as they progress from being sweet and cuddly kids to big and obnoxious teenagers.

But as I look back, it's not the big significant things that I recall – it's the small, sweet memories of two beautiful little bundles that bring me most joy.

I miss that so much.

I would give anything to re-create that moment when they first wake up and you pick them up out of bed. Or the sweet smell of their hair when they've just got dry out of the bath. Or the warmth of them in pyjamas snuggled up to you on the settee watching a film. Or the feeling of cuddling them and squeezing their little bodies and trying to resist the urge to nibble them all over.

And the total, absolute, unconditional love that they have for you as their parent.

Lottie and I share a special, undefinable bond that can only exist between father and daughter, hence the reason I decided to take this opportunity to whisk her away for both of us to spend precious time together doing Daddy / Daughter stuff before it's too late.

To me, she's still my little girl. She's still the same little bundle of joy that came in to the world just over eighteen years ago and in my eyes, she'll never grow up.

I know the passing of time is inevitable, and that I'll have to accept that she's almost a grown woman.

I also know that as I've got older and more Grumpy, and Lottie has become more worldly wise, she's already become less tolerant of my previously hilarious jokes and miserable behaviour and it won't be too long before she falls in with Wifey and sees me as a total buffoon of a man.

So, while I'm still clinging on to that last bit of Superdad status, the two of us are going away on an adventure and I'm gonna spoil her rotten. I don't care how much it costs - you can't put a value on memories.

There is also one other thing. Something that happened when Lottie was just a few weeks old that makes me and Wifey thank our lucky stars every day that she is still with us.

More of that later...

A little more about Lottie (and me)

I've just read that last chapter back and realised that that I've missed something out (this is when you, the reader, really should realise that I **am** totally winging it and that the £30.00 I spent on the half day *"How To Write Your First Novel"* probably was a total and utter waste of time and money).

I've decided to add a bit more about Lottie and me here because:

A) It's important to the book.

B) I haven't properly introduced myself and I'm a very polite person, and

C) I'd already decided that last chapter was long enough.

I'm a grumbling, grumpy old git who carries around with him over 50 years' worth of life's excess baggage and excess fat, constantly irritated by the world around me and perpetually exacerbated by the cretins that I'm forced to share my oxygen with. I have worked for over 30 years in a small, dilapidated town called Brierley Hill in the heart of the Black Country, where I have carried on the family tradition of making car parts. You probably won't know Brierley Hill but it's where they recruit the extras for that series, The Walking Dead.

I'm in a constant daily battle with rapidly growing nostril hair, a bulging waistline and an even bulgier credit card balance. I like to laugh at my own jokes, drink waaaaaaay too much gin and still hold on to the hope that one day a talent scout from Wolverhampton Wanderers will spot me at a kickabout and offer me a holding role in the centre of midfield for £50 grand a week.

Fundamentally, and like every single man of my years that you have ever met, I'm a middle-aged man with a mental age of a pre-pubescent schoolboy.

Farts make me laugh like a Minion, I love the warm fuzzy feeling that I get from alcohol and I'm obsessed with lacey bras. I tell the worst jokes, I put things on my head for a laugh and, when only Wifey is watching, swing my willy from side to side.

(If you're a woman reading this, I suspect that I've just written a pretty accurate resume of your own husband or boyfriend – trust me, we are **all** the same..).

Admittedly there are occasional moments of mild happiness in amongst the doom and gloom of daily grumpy life in the Black Country, and as I've got older

I've found that simple pleasures and the odd moral victory here and there have become the best that I can hope for.

Simple things like finding a tenner in an old pair of jeans, coming home from work and realising that you have the house all to yourself for a while and seeing someone fall over while running for a bus – these are the kind of puerile pleasures that keep me going and prove that despite being a miserable git I'm still winning at life.

Despite my grumbling, I have an affinity for Orlando and Disney that stretches back to an early age, ever since my mum and dad took me and my little sister Josie back in the late 1970's. I really loved it back then – not just because I was a wide-eyed youngster and loved Mickey Mouse, but mainly because my dad paid for it all.

Much of that holiday has been lost to me as my memory fades, buried beneath the grizzled, warped layers of adulthood. I do have a vague memory however of my dad (Don) not enjoying it very much though. He doesn't like flying for a start off so that would have caused his blood pressure to soar and his scotch intake to reach record levels and I'm pretty sure he would have had a much better time if it was just him and my mum (Mu – pronounced "Mew", short for Muriel).

My dad was tall, slim, VERY pale and proper ginger – when he took his top off at Typhoon Lagoon, he looked like a crabstick. This is obviously not the best combination to have in Florida, and probably another reason why my memory of that holiday is my dad being a proper misery - maybe that's where the Grumpy DNA comes from...

I also remember my first introduction to the Orlando weather, and my dad being petrified of being caught out in an electrical storm (not surprising really as we'd never seen one in Dudley).

It didn't help that we stayed in Disney's Contemporary Resort, you know, the Toblerone shaped one with the monorail going through the middle. My dad was totally convinced that as soon as he got on that monorail it was gonna be struck by lightning. I can hear him now...

"Mew. Mew! I ay gooin on that god monorail! It ay safe!"

Mind you, this was the 70's so me dad was pretty much wearing 100% polyester clothing, even his pants. I reckon if he'd have walked quickly across The Contemporary Resort carpet, he would have created his own private electrical storm.

Anyway, fast forward 4 decades and it's me playing the role of my dad and I get to take my own little Fam to the most magically expensive place on earth. We've been together as a family three times in the last 6 years before this trip and have created some wonderfully expensive memories. Luckily, Lottie and I share the same wide-eyed wonder for all things Disney and out of the four of us, we are the softest by a Black Country mile. So, it was an easy decision for me, having Lottie to be my sole travelling companion for this latest adventure.

Lottie has a very quirky sense of humour. She is ridiculously quick-witted, finds something funny in most situations, and invents catchphrases and sayings that leave me and Wifey in both bewilderment and fits of giggles. She can be quite cutting with her sense of humour too, and more often than not the old crumbly parents are the butt of her teenage humour.

Truth is, she's always been like it, ever since she was a little girl.

For instance, when she was about 6, she used to play "Shops" with Wifey in the bathroom – as Wifey had a long, luxurious soak in the bath, Lottie would wander in pretending to be the old shopkeeper, open the airing cupboard door and pretend that all the items in it were for sale. They spent hours and hours bartering over the contents of the cupboard, where Lottie would pretend that everything was available at the right price.

"I don't suppose you've got... I bet you haven't have ya.... Errrrm have you got any toothpaste? I only want half a tube though!" Wifey would ask.

"You're in luck me wench! I've got exactly half a tube", Lottie the Shopkeep would channel her inner Mrs Overall and reply in an old croaky voice. "You can have it for 6 pence my luv. I'll wrap it up for ya".

This game would go on interspersed with fits of giggles with leftover shampoo, battered toothbrushes, plastic bath toys and all manner of random plumbing items being sold for a song. Eventually, when Lottie The Shopkeep had sold off everything, Wifey would get out of the bath and send her giggling happily in to bed.

One day, running out of things to buy in the cupboard, Wifey asked:

"Eerrr... I don't suppose you've got an airing cupboard door have ya?".

"Oooh, I haven't got one of those spare my luv. It'll be in next Tuesday" croaked Lottie The Shopkeep as she licked the end of an imaginary pencil and wrote down the order on an imaginary notepad, followed by more giggles from the pair of them.

Eventually, Lottie went off happily and snugly to bed and Wifey disappeared downstairs to watch more Alan Titchmarsh programmes and drink gin.

A couple of days later, we were out in the car on our way to the shops when from the back-seat Lottie said:

"Mum, what day is it?".

"Today is Tuesday, Lottie. All day!".

There was a few moments silence, broken by Lottie who stared out of the car window and said:

"Oh good. Your door will be in when we get back".

And that's how she's always been – a good old Black Country mixture of potty, quirky, zany and bonkers. A perfectly beautiful bundle of a human being with very funny bones.

Another delightful trait that Lottie has is a total absence of any kind of filter between the random thoughts that gather in her head and her voice box. This has led to many instances over the years when the most delightful, randomly innocent, ridiculous thoughts just spurt out of her mouth which, for obvious future comedy purposes, I've saved on my phone.

In the Grumpy household, these have become known as "Lottie Logic" and I'm delighted to offer you a few gems below.

A struggle with names and places...

Is Jim short for Jimothy?

Who is Israel?

I thought Dick van Dyke was a painter

Is Jim short for Jimathon, then?

Is Cuba called Cuba because it's a cube?

What do they speak in Switzerland? Hollandaise?

You can't speak Danish. It's a pastry.

Random stuff about animals...

Can emo's fly?

Dogs don't have chins.

Prawn crackers are made out of baby prawn eggs.

Can you post a dog?

Isn't sparrow a vegetable?

Do wood pigeons burn easily?

And a final mixture of Lottie Logics...

Could you go on Countdown if you're dyslexic?

Wouldn't you love to be inside the dishwasher when it's switched on?

Now you've opened a can of beans......

You know if you plant a spliff, can you grow weed?

You can't die standing up.

Is paraplegic a bleach?

You can't eat a sundae on a Tuesday.

Is a breadwinner like a competition for vegetables?

All true and all totally random, just like Lottie.

So, there you have it. I reckon I have completed the task of introducing the main characters so maybe it wasn't the worst £30.00 I've ever spent. Housekeeping over, let's rock and roll to the next chapter – the pre-holiday diet!

Before we go any further, there is one other thing... something that I eluded to in the previous chapter.

On Thursday July 20th, 2000 at around eight thirty in the morning, an ambulance arrived at my house. Shortly after, a paramedic carried my precious little Lottie in to it and rushed her to the hospital.

She was pale, listless and on the verge of losing her short life.

Overnight she had developed an illness, the symptoms of which were nothing unusual but just a bit... strange. She was quiet, subdued and wouldn't feed. She kept falling asleep and was hardly moving.

It was difficult to know what to do, so as young parents we did what we thought was right - we just cuddled her and put her to bed, not realising that with every passing second our little baby girl was beginning a fight to save her own life.

We now know that Lottie had contracted meningitis, and over the course of the next horrific 3 weeks, we would be perilously close to losing her.

If I ever need more reason to seize every single precious moment with my beautiful daughter, I just think back to that time when she was at death's door.

A poor, lifeless infant.

A small, pale bundle of skin and bones.

My Lottie, almost lost to the world before she had chance to make the world and everyone in it realise what a remarkable human being she is.

So that's what I decided to do with this trip. To make as many memories as I can with my beautiful daughter while we both have the chance, and to relay her story to as many people as possible so they can see a tiny bit of the Lottie that I see.

Fatty frustration and the art of the binge diet

There is a pivotal moment long before any holiday that both male and female Grumpies will be familiar with. It's a sudden, shocking moment that hits you when you least expect it. A moment of sadness, anger and despair and usually ending in blubbery tears.

The "moment" can be one of two things but has the same devastating effect on both pride and ego. It can happen when you unexpectedly catch sight of yourself in the mirror or take an unflattering selfie. Or it could be when you go to try on a new item of clothing in your size and can barely get it past your belly, bum or thighs.

The "moment" is of course when you realise that since you last had your flesh out on holiday, you've had 10 months of grazing on take-aways whilst burying your head in the sand and your gym gear in the bottom of the wardrobe and it's finally caught up with your chubby self.

You need to go on a pre-holiday diet.

I'm forever doing this, trapped in a cycle of weight gain and binge dieting. Probably since my early thirties actually, which was the last time that any fashionable clothes fitted me properly. Funnily enough, that coincides with the arrival of my two kids and the chaotic non-sleeping, crap-eating lifestyle that they bring home with them from the maternity ward.

Their arrival also heralded the departure of many other of my physical pastimes like playing football, golf, and my absolute favourite, Bedtime Twister with Wifey.

Me: "OK, I'll spin. Your right hand, red. Now, my left foot blue."

Wifey: "Why have you taken your clothes off?"

Me: "Ssssh... you'll see. You've got to put both hands on yellow now love, face down and stay perfectly still"

Wifey: "OOOOHH! I say! I didn't expect that. Is that in the rules?"

I know I'm on common ground here as I've seen all the Facebook posts about weight loss and the associated dilemmas. Let's face it, if you are a little, ahem, on the larger side, Orlando is probably not the best place to be heading to spend your hard-earned summer holiday.

I don't want to offend any of you fatties that are reading, so I'll just speak from my own experience here. I absolutely love my food and I am such a greedy guts, and this truly is a lethal combination in Orlando. There is way too much temptation for an overeating chubby like me, especially as I like to get my money's worth, have no backbone and my "FULL" button doesn't seem to work.

None of this is helped by the size of the food portions in Orlando.

On a typical Orlando day, for breakfast you could have pancakes stacked up like roof tiles plastered with maple syrup, for lunch a burger so high that they have to stick a bamboo cane through it to stop it falling over and dislocate your jaw to eat it and for tea you could have a pizza the size of a manhole cover accompanied by unlimited salad.

Yeah, unlimited salad - like that's gonna help.

Orlando salad is not like that pathetic salad "cart" that they have at the Dudley Harvester where you get a bowl the size of an egg cup and try to cram everything in so you end up with a stodgy mess of limp lettuce, shredded carrot, sweetcorn and kidney beans (Uh? Kidney beans? Who's going out for a meal and **choosing** to eat kidney beans?). All of which is plastered in sickly thousand island sauce. Orlando salad bars are as long as an artic lorry and have a wide variety of food on offer, including bread, rice, pasta, cake, chocolate, vegetables, chips, eggs, meat and cheese. Sometimes they even have salad.

When you've finished, you can take the pizza "to go" just in case you get hungry next week and then wobble over to The Cheesecake Factory for dessert.

Well, we've all got a separate dessert stomach, right?

This is a famous Orlando specialist pudding restaurant, very well-known and popular to the UK members of various Facebook sites and the only restaurant I've ever known to have a permanent defibrillation team on standby.

Funnily enough, The Cheesecake Factory specialises in cheesecake and has a choice of about 500 different coloured ones that all basically taste the same. Each one is about the size of a plane chock and just 5 mouthfuls would be your total calorie allowance for a week.

On top of all that, every meal is washed down with dustbin sized beakers of sugary drinks in all manner of different colours and flavours, each one containing a potentially lethal combination of man-made chemicals. I've noticed a pattern here – all these drinks promise an immediate return for each gulpy investment, either by a sudden, dramatic improvement to your mental condition by way of an adrenaline fuelled boost or the stamina, performance and body of a top athlete. I mean, seriously, who drinks Gatorade and thinks that it's doing them any good? You might just as well drink Harpic.

I know I'm totally and utterly biased, but my trusty sidekick and soon-to-be-suffering travelling companion Lottie always looks great, so there's another reason for getting myself into shape. Lottie has an effortless beauty, which she obviously gets from Wifey, great taste in clothes, which she obviously gets from Wifey, and she's fab at putting on makeup, which she obviously gets from me. Thankfully, she's skipped that young lady stage where it seems compulsory to share the hips back, tits out, pouty faced pictures with the rest of the pervy world on Snapchat and Instagram.

However, along with every other teenage girl she is obsessed with her eyebrows. I apologise if you are reading this and you too are permanently preoccupied by making sure your eyebrows look like they've been drawn on with a marker pen, but what on earth is the point? Who wants two big commas for eyebrows and a facial expression that is one of permanent surprise? I know I'm old and grumpy and not exactly down with the kids these days but surely this is the most ridiculous fashion craze ever.

Knowing she's gonna look a million dollars every day is added pressure to up my game in order to avoid following her around looking like some fat middle aged stalky tramp.

And because I want to look my best in case I get spotted.

Writing the book, creating my own blog page and generally being a dick on Orlando Facebook sites or 12 months has led to a very low level of notoriety. Of course, my Black Country mates have been quick to seize on this and I've become known as "The Bard of Bilston" or the "Wolverhampton Wordsworth". And they're the polite ones.

Before the holiday the possibility of being spotted had been mentioned by The Fam. In fact, it had become the subject of a bet with my stake confidently wagered on the probability that I **would** be recognised, not just once but **at least 5 times** during our stay. With an equal amount of confidence, Lottie went for zero.

So, faced with the nightmare dilemma of arriving fat and leaving fatter, and maybe having a fan comment that I'm chubbier in real life than they thought, I decided yet again to try to slim down a dress size before the trip and try another crash diet.

I've done em all before. The one I tried this time was snazzily titled:

"Let's try to defy the laws of physics and fly in the face of logic by trying to lose 2 stones in less than 3 weeks so I can fit in my holiday clothes" diet.

I think. It may actually have been called the "Dukan" or "Atkins", I don't remember exactly. What I do know is that each one of these faddy diets are all accompanied by rabid constipation and rank bad breath as you're only allowed to eat food that corks your bumhole up and causes you to have the breath of a 1000 festival portaloos.

Whichever one it was, it was pretty much the same diet as the one I was on before we went to Orlando last year and ended up with me putting on 2 stones, so that went well, didn't it?

Fundamentally, my main problem is will power, of which I have fuck all.

Even when I'm trying **really** hard, the merest culinary temptation sees me crack like an egg. Take the other night for example. On my way back from a footie match, I'm happily looking at the football results on my phone in the back of Teenage Son's car when I noticed we had made a sudden left turn. I looked up to see if we had turned into our road, but as it happened we had stopped outside the local chippy.

My mate who was in the front seat was feeling a bit peckish, so he'd asked my boy if we could stop for some chips on the way back. As we pulled up he said in a Black Country accent:

"Am yow havin' any chips Mike?"

"Nah" I said, "I'm on a diet. Tryin to be good, ay I?"

I'm not sure what happened next, but quicker than you can say Michelle McManus I'm standing in the chip shop with my nostrils full off the heady whiff of fat and vinegar, ordering a large bag of yellow battered chips, curry sauce and a jar of cockles. I'd convinced myself that the cockles would count as one of my five a day, making them the one of the day I'd actually had.

Back home, the chips were delicately placed on to a slice of bleached white bread that had been smeared with butter, lathered in curry sauce and then folded over like a chunky Cornish pasty before being crammed into my chubby face.

It was delicious.

And that's the problem. As soon as my will power evaporates, my dieting conscious falls through a fatman sized trapdoor and I find myself caving in, ending up eating more than before.

If only you could buy a back bone… Mind you, knowing me it'd be deep fried and eaten with mash.

The best bit of advice I have ever had was from a sage old Black Country bloke I know who'd noticed that I'd put on a bit of timber.

"Ya know what yower problem is young Michael?"

"No", says young Michael (that's me, by the way)

"The ole at the top is bigger than the ole at the bottom"

Wise words, I'm sure you'll agree.

Despite my lack of will power I did try to be good in the weeks running up to the holiday and did cut down on the nice things that I enjoy, make me happy and make life worth living.

Man, I was miserable in those few weeks.

For example, I cut my gin intake to just a bottle every other day and stopped adding the fattening tonic all together. Also, on my daily waddle from work to Brierley Hill post office, I purposely avoided Poundland where you can buy 3 sellotaped together Kinder Buenos for a quid. A quid!

And, as luck would have it, Greggs burned down.

This automatically removed the temptation for a lukewarm floppy sausage roll on my walk back. The fire at Greggs didn't stop Brierley Hill's finest trying to loot it **as it was still in flames**, with some chavs running out with armfuls of steak bakes and still complaining they weren't hot enough.

(Greggs never did re-open, which is a crying shame as if ever there is a town with the perfect demographic for fatty, pork n cheese based savoury snacks and donuts it's Brierley Hill. When it was opened in the precinct a few years ago, Greggs was initially viewed as some sort of new-fangled, posh, health food delicatessen "loike they 'ave in Berminghum" and the locals, who had previously lived on a diet of faggots, beef dripping sandwiches and scratchings, eyed it with nervous suspicion. And it's easy to understand why in some respects, especially as the daily stock of pork pies doubled the whole towns IQ. It must be difficult for a Brierley Hillbilly to accept that you have less chromosomes than a Greggs pork pie).

Try as I might, and as is always the case, the holiday diet went out of the window as it got too close to make any difference (about 2 weeks beforehand) and I resigned myself to going over to the Land of Scoff in the shape that I was already in – namely that of a bowling pin.

Now, if one of those Beardy Branson Trolley Dollies asks me if I want one of this seatbelt extenders, I'm gonna kick off...

The chapter about the trying on of holiday clothes and wishing you'd stuck to the binge diet

The time for Lottie and I to depart was edging ever closer so it was time to get up the loft once again, blow the cobwebs off the cases and sort out the holiday clobber.

It would help if I could actually see the God cases once I'm up there. Our loft is like a hoarder's paradise and the cases and holiday clobber are buried under an avalanche of stuff that should have been chucked in the bin years ago. The problem is, Wifey won't throw <u>anything</u> away, especially if it has a connection to the kids growing up.

Dolls with eyes missing, broken toy trucks, saggy knitted characters, knackered pushchairs... We've got the lot up our loft. I swear we have more kids' clothes than Mothercare and we could start up and trade for years on our own online toys shop. She keeps everything and refuses to throw it away, from baby grows to ballet shoes and Thomas The Tank Engine tat to Transformers.

And we have a worrying collection of children body parts too...

A first tooth in a jewellery box.

A lock of hair in a sandwich bag.

A collection of toenails in a Tupperware container.

Flakes of skin in an envelope.

An eyeball in a jar.

(I might have made that last one up).

It does puzzle me why Wifey keeps all these bits of child. What's she gonna do with them?

My theory is that when they've left home and she's stuck with just me for company, she's going to build two effigies of Sam and Lottie out of Papier Mache. Then she's going to glue the teeth, hair, toenails and skin back on and sit them in the kitchen and chat while she pretends to cook tea.

After 30 irritated, painful minutes of shuffling stuff about the loft, banging my head and repeatedly stepping on hidden bits of Lego, the cases and the holiday clothes eventually burst angrily through the hatch and fell down to the landing, ready for the next phase – the trying on.

I admit I'm the hoarder when it comes to holiday clothes and I bought down a couple of cases from the loft stuffed full of really nice holiday gear, most of which I'm never, ever going to wear. This is mainly due to two reasons:

1 – I've come to terms with the fact that printed silk shirts, kimonos and drop crotch trousers aren't a good look for a man of my years.

2 – As I've got older, my body has plumped up as gracefully as a slowly filling helium balloon, rendering many of the holiday clothes that I bought back in the day (Salou, 1986 being a particular high point) totally useless unless you have a size 28 waist, a six pack and cornrows.

Anyhow, in my head I still think I'm 18 and I'm convinced the mirror is faulty, you know, like one of those ones you see at the funfair that makes your head look as distortedly big as Ant McPartlins. So it doesn't stop me from having a go at trying most stuff on, whole-heartedly believing that I can carry it off by correcting my slouch, sucking my belly in and pushing my shoulders back.

I can't.

My flabby situation isn't helped at all by the fact that the faulty mirror in question is full length and on the landing, meaning I get a full on chubby view of myself each time I go upstairs.

I hate that mirror.

There are occasions when it's not too bad, for example if I leave the landing light off and squint. I've found that immediately sheds pounds. But most of the time it's still me and not David Gandy looking magnificently back in tight white boxers and a washboard stomach.

It does occasionally get me down – the lack of willpower combined with the inevitable passing of time means I will never be thin, and that does upset me.

One night, after a particularly tough session trying on new TK Maxx shirts which ended in more chubby tears, I decided once and for all to take matters into my own hands and finally get in control of my **own** destiny.

To be strong and decide who's in charge – **me or the food?**

To realise that body shaming myself is not good for my fragile ego and it's time **I did something about it**.

So, I went in to my shed, got my biggest hammer and smashed the fucking mirror to pieces.

That did the trick and I think I looked alright in my pink cheesecloth shirt and white linen capri pants with red piping. Well, I think I did as I couldn't really see as I'd smashed the mirror up, but it seemed to get a reaction when I popped out shopping later that day. The Aldi mums were agog!

The problem with being a bit chubby at my age and sporting moobs like a two leaky kiddies water balloons has been further exacerbated recently as my favourite clothes shop, Mark and Spencer's decided to employ a new, trendy German clothes designer called Fitz Nicentight and almost immediately all the shirts were labelled "*Slim Fit*"

** shudders **

Those two words strike fear into otherwise hunky blokes like me.

When did "*Slim Fit*" become a thing? And why wasn't I and my chubby brethren consulted?

Who in their right mind thinks that "*Slim Fit*" is a good way to sell clothes to flabby men? And when did you ever see anyone that looks "slim fit" shopping in Marks and Spencers?

You didn't.

Cos they don't.

Cos they all shop in Top Man.

Skinny bastards.

When I go in to Marks and Spencers, I feel like a young, spritely buck compared to all the other crusty old farts shopping in the beige section, so I feel rightly hard done to that more than half the clothes in there are designed for people too young to remember when St Michael was trendy.

Me and Marks and Spencer go way back - I've still got some old jumpers with the St Michael labels in the collar. Back in the 70's, we were dead posh and my mum used to buy all my school clothes from M & S as it saved on sewing name tags. Nothing but the best for mummy's little Black Country soldier.

But along with the slim fit shirts, something else must have changed in the design office as their clothes don't seem to fit me anymore. Where there used to be a wide range of clothes to choose from, now everything seems to be that little bit more snug.

This is nothing to do with the fact that I've been steadily grazing on fatty food and sugary drinks, whilst simultaneously doing no exercise whatsoever for the last few years, or that I've grown my own blubber flotation device around the middle of my body. Nothing to do with that at all.

I'm telling ya, there's been a design change caused by cutbacks so they're using less material than before. And elasticated waistbands are expensive to make...

Another item of clothing that I neither asked for nor understand from M & S is moleskin trousers.

Moleskin. Who wants to wear moleskin?

And why?

What's next? Gerbil pants? Hamster boxers? (Although I bet Richard Gere has a pair).

How many moles does it take to make a pair of trousers? I've seen a mole and they're tiny, so it must take at least a couple hundred just for one leg.

I bet Marks and Spencers have got their own free range mole farm, where all the moles are organically and ethically bred and to maximise profits they put the rest of the skinned mole in them posh tapas pots and pretend it's Peri Peri Chicken.

Speaking of moles, we have a guy who comes round our house to "catch" the moles whenever we get sudden big piles of fresh dirt appearing in the garden.

Wifey calls him up and sure enough next day "**Dave The Mole Man**" appears with all manner of moley gadgets, most of which look like bent pieces of scrap metal that he's found in a skip that he's now pretending to be the latest technology in mole entrapment.

He pokes these bits of tat in the fresh piles of dirt and promises to come back in a few days. Lo and behold, would you believe it, when he returns he's only gone and caught one!

One.

I know this as he insists on either showing us a dead mole, or if we've gone out he sends Wifey the pictures on WhatsApp.

Well, I think it's a mole…

It is a bit gruesome, seeing these mangled up bits of short sighted mammal, but it's his proof that the bent bits of scrap metal have done their job and a sort of a receipt for his services (£10 per dead mole).

Thinking about it, I wouldn't recognise one mole from another. For all I know, Dave The Mole Man might have a collection of stuffed moles that he shows off to his gullible suburban wife customers. He could be a complete mole-catching charlatan, touring the districts of the Black Country placing piles of freshly dug soil in posh back gardens in the dead of night, awaiting an emergency call on the Mole Hotline next day so he can rush round with his collection of scrap metal gadgets and then come back in 24 hours showing off pictures of a taxidermied mole with his eyes closed and his tongue sticking out.

If I were sending the pictures, I'd be arranging the moles in a more dramatic death pose, you know, like having one with both diggy hands clutched to his heart or maybe hands clasped together on their knees in a sort "pray for forgiveness" kinda pose.

That's what I'd do. But then I'm not right in the head.

Anyway, back to the story and I'm telling ya now, **sort yourself out Marks N Sparks**, or I'll go back to shopping at British Home Stores… you have been warned.

After a few days of trying on shirts that made me look like I was trying to kneed spam into a lycra bag, and shorts that made it obvious which side I dress, I managed to scrape enough clothes to pass as a fully functioning human being in Orlando and they were chucked in the case along with the compulsory Grumpy T Shirt and Grumpy pyjama bottoms.

By contrast, Lottie effortlessly chucks any clothes on and immediately looks amazing, leading me to believe that I may spend a lot of my time in Orlando looking like a very scruffy, over-protective bodyguard.

Travel day

*The Travel Day Chapter is brought to you by **Smirnoff Vodka and Apple Juice**, the number 1 choice of scaredy cat travellers!!*

Due to missing several hair appointments at Shaky Bobs in the run up to this Floriday, I awoke this morning at FOUR AM with what can only be described as Boris Johnson hair. You know, the kind of sticky up, wild bed-head hair where you look like you've been dragged through a hedge backwards. Or had to escape quickly from under the quilt of a married woman's bedroom.

Alas, I cannot offer you photographic evidence of this hair-raising disaster although, like Boris, today I have a strong urge to leave Europe.

After a cup of sweet, black coffee followed by a bleary eyed shower, I successfully completed the transformation from Caveman Boris to World Travelling Ponce, and in no time at all Lottie and I were waving goodbye to the other 50% of The Fam as we jumped in to the taxi. As soon as the cases were in the boot and the doors of the Skoda Estate slammed shut, Molly the Cockapoo was already lying on my side of the bed with a cheeky smirk and Wifey had laid out my best gins in readiness for her 8-night, snore-free Candy Crushing marathon.

Anyhoo, off we hurtled up the M6, motoring through such wonderful towns as... Bilston... Stoke... Congleton (which I always think sounds like something off a kids programme, like Camberwick Green) and Nantwich. These Midlandish provincial names were soon to be swapped with Celebration, Davenport, Kissimmee and Orlando.

Wowzer. I was excited.

Our driver for this jaunt through the delightful roadworks of the M6 was a guy called George. A nice enough chap but he was older than God's dog, possessed the longest nostril hair I have ever seen in my entire life, and was a bit twitchy on the old pedals, both managing to simultaneously brake and accelerate at the same time, which made it an interestingly jerky ride as i twyed ti rite.

It also appeared that George may have just had new dentures, probably ill fitted by Shaky Bob's brother, Trembly Fred the Dudley Dentist, so when he sssspoke he ssssorta whisssstled lotssss through the gapssss in hissss teethsssss.

As we wound our way through traffic cones, this amused me for a few miles as I tried to get him to unwittingly answer my questions like:

"How far we got left, George?"

"Sssthixsssty sssthisssx milessssth"

"What's the next place to get a coffee George?"

"Ssssandbach ssservices"

And "What phone you got George?"

"A Sssthmassssung Ssss Sssixsss"

It killed 10 minutes. I knew I had to sssstop when George got a bit funny when I asked him if he knew the name of the girl who sssellsss sssea ssshells on the ssssea sssshore and when Lottie asked if ssshe could hear a kettle whisssling. I imagine all the dogs in Congleton had got a bit tetchy too.

Sssafely deposited by Whistling George at Manchester Airport Terminal 2, we checked in our cases and headed off to security to be met with a massive queue. It must have been going on for a while as the mums and dads already had that pissed off "Jesus Christ I've got this for two weeks" look and their little kids were causing total chaos and mayhem by running off, hiding, sliding along the floor and getting several days' worth of dust and germs all over their new holiday clothes.

It must be a Manc name I've not heard before, as a lot of these kids were called "Gerreeeya". One of them must have been a bit posher as she had a double barrel name "Gerreeeya-Naaaaa".

We eventually shuffled toward the front of the queue and it appeared that the hold up had been caused by the body scanning machine breaking down - you know the one where you have to stand in the big microwave machine and copy the outlined "Stick 'em up!" pose so the perverts behind the telly can get a good gawp at your underwear?

Trust me, that's all it's for.

Guns and explosives my arse...

In order to get the queues shifting, some Manc security guards had decided to ditch the idea of underwear scanning and instead had just chalk drawn a silhouette on a blank wall in the shape of a bloke dabbing. Thus ensued a line of happy holiday makers lining up to dab and being cheered on by their fellow holiday makers and uniformed blokes who should really have been checking to see if any naughty ragamuffin had smuggled TNT in their underpants.

Dab completed in style and happy that no machine had secretly x rayed my perky bottom, we shuffled off to find the posh lounge. Lottie had pre-booked this on my say so, purely because it works out financially better to pay a one off £20.00 than pay Mr Wetherspoon £60.00 for the equivalent of a bacon roll and 6 large vodkas.

I had a slight shock when she told me she'd booked "The Escape Lounge", leading me to temporarily believe we were to take part in some sort of covert operation where you pay a small fortune for a grown up game of Hide and Seek – just what I need as my anxiety levels are about to peak at the thought of being stuck in a plane for 8 hours.

As it happens, it's a posh(ish) private room full of greedy people like me who have all paid a nominal amount of money to push their limit on gluttony. In the 90 minutes or so before you board the plane, upon which you will be plied with alcohol and stodgy food, you can merrily drink your own body weight in booze, steal all the posh magazines and snaffle the mini muffins wrapped up in stolen napkins.

Lottie and I settled down and as I worked out a way to nick an entire tray of flapjacks for the flight, she stuck her headphones in and monged out.

Lottie does this a lot. Sometimes, I can be talking to her for a good five minutes before I realise she's not listening to me but Tinie Tempah or Jazzy B Bookcase or whatever these crazy cats listen to these days.

When she's in my company, she also puts her headphones in to block out the noise of my chewing. Lottie pretends to suffer from a condition called *Misophonia*, which is broadly defined as a "hatred of sound", where negative emotions, thoughts, and physical reactions are triggered by specific noises.

In Lottie's case, the specific noise is her old man chobbling on his food.

Mealtimes in our house are a nightmare, especially if I'm having pork scratchings or crackling which, being from The Black Country, I do every night obviously. That and turnips, which are our local delicacy. As soon as we start sit down for a meal, I sense her eyes on me as I chew, chobble, crunch and generally mash my lips, tongue and teeth around.

And that's just when I'm eating soup.

It's got so bad that depending on what we're eating we have to time our bites and chews so she can't get so annoyed at me. This involves looking at each other and trying to take equal bites of the same food at precisely the same time, without laughing. Our synchronised eating must be comical to watch for Wifey and Sam and has become known in the Grumpy household as a "Choff Off".

One time we were totally out of synch and eating risotto. Halfway through Lottie slammed her fork down and, in a theatrical manner which only Teenage girls have ever perfected, threw her head back in irritated exasperation.

"Fuh God's sake Dad!!! Have you got blunt teeth? How can you **chew** _risotto_?"

With the amount of time we have together and the number of meals we have planned, I reckon Lottie may well have her headphones permanently in over the next eight days...

After a curled up bacon sarnie and a few cheeky snifters, I staggered off for a whissstle ssstop tour of duty free to obtain some more cheeky in-flight vodka and apple juice and to see how much W H Smith charge for Maltesers.

£2.99! I only paid a quid at Dudley Asda yesterday!

Rant alert - Is there a more soul-destroying experience in travel history than having to buy something from an airport W H Smith?

I hate that shop with a vengeance. When did Mr W H Smith think it was a good idea to get rid of all his counter staff and replace them with shit robots AT THE BUSIEST AIRPORTS IN THE COUNTRY? These self-scan machines in shops are utter bastards and should be immediately outlawed (If I'm ever Prime Minister that's the first thing I'm gonna do. That and make Holly Willoughby Queen forever).

Every experience I've ever had with a self-scan is totally and utterly soul destroying – either my bag hasn't been registered, my banana is the wrong length (stop it...) or I scan something and "**Please wait, shop assistance is required**" belts out from the back of the machine.

The W H Smith's ones are simply the worst ever though. They are the Simon Cowell of self-scan machines – irritating, arrogant, pompous and a total waste of mine and everybody's time.

They're about as much use as tits on a fish.

For a start off, everything in the shop is way too expensive and costs twice as much just cos you're in an airport and the greedy bastards have you by the short n curlies.

Then there's always a long, bad tempered queue as some confused old biddy in massive beige elasticated trousers has no clue how to use the scanner, causing a tailback that snakes all the way to the double-priced Kinder Bueno stand at the back of the shop.

Then when you do eventually get to a machine that's actually working and start scanning, it asks in a stuck-up voice to see your boarding pass!

Why? What the fuck's it got to do with you where I'm going you tinny voiced, arrogant nosey twat?

I only want a bottle of apple juice.

I managed to complete my task and gave the machine a swift kick before I left (I always do that. Always), noticing as I went that the old lady in the mahoosive beige trousers was now leaning down and trying to explain in to the scanner that she's left her boarding pass with her husband.

Apple juice safely tucked in my backpack, it was time to get Vodka so off I went to Duty Free for a heady whiff of Coco Mademoiselle or a cheeky spray of Old Spice. Or a 3 foot long Toblerone.

As previously mentioned, the thought had crossed my mind that I MIGHT be recognised and I guessed that a busy airport packed with Fams all jetting off for their own magical holiday would be a prime meeting spot for Facebook Folk. Judging by the number of people with those personalised family t shirts sporting Mickey Ears and slogans like "Disney Dad" (barf) "We finish each other's...Sandwiches" (hurl) and "Mummy's Little Princess" (aaah, that's cute) I assumed that there must be a fair few people who may have read my blogs.

Being the unassuming, humble kinda guy what I am, I have no idea how I'd react if someone did approach me. I mean, it's not like I've been practising my autograph or finding my best profile for selfies or anything...

So I'm slightly squiffy from the booze I've already had and I'm in the queue to pay for a Take Away Vodka in Duty Free when I notice a rather attractive looking lady just behind me, looking at me in a funny kinda way. You know when you can tell from their body language that someone wants to speak to you, but they can't find the right moment?

Yeah?

Well it was like that.

I smiled at her in a sort of "Kuh, this queue eh?" kinda way to give her the opportunity to say hello.

It worked!

She leaned in towards me and with a smiley look that I took for recognition said

"Excuse me. Are you Michael Hadley?"

This was it! I'd been recognised!

I'D FINALLY MADE IT!

My mind was immediately filled with wonderful thoughts and images. Before me lay a glittering literary career, laced with hot chicks, fame and fortune. I could see big film deals and headlining chat shows. Maybe a Pulitzer or an OBE for my services to charity.

Or a knighthood?? Who knows? I bet the Queen would love my blogs, they're right up her Pall Mall.

So, I fluttered my eyes, looked fondly at said lovely lady and in my nicest, poshest Black Country accent said:

"Yes, it's me love. I **am** Michael Hadley. Guess you must have seen my stuff on Facebook. Would you like a selfie?"

As I giddily reached for my phone to record the moment for prosperity, she replied:

"No mate, you've dropped your passport "

Realising I'm not even a poor man's Phillip Schofield I crashed down to earth with an embarrassing bump, and returned in shame to The Escape Lounge. After I'd found Lottie hiding behind a desk and shoved 3 more Danish Pastries in me back pocket, we bid bonjour to the friendly staff and headed off to the gate as our flight was boarding.

Just the thought of the display changing to "Flight boarding" is enough to send me in to a nervy meltdown.

Some of you may know from the first book that I'm scared of flying so I have to reach a certain level of mashed before I feel happy enough to strap myself into a flammable tube with 4 highly combustible engines. This does involve a Michael Hadley Style Cocktail which I won't describe for fear of being banned from Virgin Atlantic - suffice to say that it works for me and transforms me into a much dopier, relaxed and soppy version of myself.

Once on board we did the traditional Facebook "It's Our Turn" picture for all my fans and despite my drunken efforts I failed miserably in getting enough support to lead my fellow passengers in a sing song of "It's A Small World After All..."

My cocktail of booze and drugs does turn me into a massive, doe-eyed softie and I confess that I did get emotional as we took off. Me and my little girl were heading for a fabulous adventure together, and the moment that the engine roared down the runway and the wheels left planet earth was when it hit me – we'd really started on our journey.

As we zoomed up in to the grey Manchester sky and burst through rain filled clouds, I held tightly on to Lottie's hand and taken back to a time when she was really little and just as scared of flying as I am now. To calm her down I used to play a daft card game with her, a bit like Snap but called "Spotty Dog" where you had to find the matching spotty pooches at each turn of a card. We used to laugh and laugh as I pretended to be silly and get all the spotty dogs mixed up, and she'd giggle at her daft dad whilst shuffling the cards with her little hands...

I looked at her with a tear in my eye as she pushed her headphones further in (I'd just opened a packet of mini pretzels) and I was reminded that she's still that same girl. I could not be any prouder of the young woman she's turning in to, but my god I miss her being little.

I booze-snoozed a little and only awoke when I heard the delightful chink of the drinks trolley getting closer. Trust me on this, there are few more attractive sights or sounds in the world to a drunken traveller than the wondrous appearance of a well-stocked drinks trolley, staffed by a gorgeous woman in a tight-fitting uniform.

Corrrrr...

Fair play to Mr Branson, he's employed the bounciest, poppiest, fluffiest girls on planet earth to serve drinks and hot food to scruffy, drunken chavellers like me.

Aren't they delightful? Just when you're at your worst, pickled drunk with gin dribbled down your shirt and pretzel crumbs on your beard, they appear by your side, sweet smelling, curvy and alluring to ask if you'd like another pillow behind your head or maybe some help with the TV.

My god...

The trouble is, in my inebriated state I just smile dopily back and say yes to everything on offer.

Which is why I got banned from British Airways, although First Officer Winton does stay in touch.

The flight passed in seemingly no time – I constantly embarrassed Lottie, the food was ace, the drinks flowed and the buxom service was delightful. Ten outta ten Beardy Branson, even I can't moan.

It was a bit bumpy as we came in to land but that's to be expected with the infamous Orlando bi-polar weather and the heat radiating off all those kiddy temper tantrums going on down below. Grumpy tip - tell the kids it's scientifically proven that all those hot, salty tears and snot bubbles are eating away at the ozone layer and it's their own future they're ruining. That'll stop em.

As the plane touched down on the Florida tarmac and we came to a standstill, I could already feel my entire body breathe a sigh of relief and relax – we'd made it!

Hard Rock here we come!

Day 1 - Hard Rock

Well, I say Day 1. It's really day *minus* 1. Due to the time difference that exists between Dudley and Orlando, we landed just 4 chronological hours after we took off, which is not bad for an 8 hour flight.

I wonder what I did in those missing 4 hours? Mind you, I've been so smacked off my tits on booze and tranquilisers I could have lost or gained an entire day for all I know. Halfway through the flight I'd somehow managed to tie my flight socks together and woke up wearing them like a blindfold – I have no memory of doing this.

Anyhow, by the time we arrived there was still enough hours left to class it as a "holiday day" if you know what I mean, so for the sake of the episodic nature of the book I'll stick to calling it Day 1 for all you pedanticks out their.

Freed from the confines and fetid air of the plane (and massively relieved to be using my passport as identification rather than The Fam having to call Trembly Fred the Dudley Dentist for my dental records) I bounced out of the door and cheekily skipped up the ramp like a happy toddler let off the reins for the first time.

Due to my inebriated state, I had to be guided through the arrivals bit and out towards US Immigration by a very patient Lottie. I simultaneously giggled and trumped all the way, my face bright red and with my head bobbing about like a loose shirt button. Lottie gently steered and cajoled me along, stopping me from walking up the wrong side of the travellator and catching me just in time before I used the lady's loos.

She's doing a great job already, my apprentice carer.

We bumbled our way through the arrivals maze and joined the throngs of exhausted travellers at US Immigration, all patiently waiting for their turn to be screened by the hardnosed customs guys whilst desperately resisting the urge to do anything suspicious or look at their phones for fear of being hoiked outta line and told off by Police Officer Dibble on the US Federal Government naughty step.

Now, believe me, I'm squeaky clean readers and I've never broken the law back home but there's something about these US Customs guys that unnerves me.

Maybe it's the way they ask the questions or stare at you, but I always feel incredibly intimidated and, for some inexplicable reason, insanely guilty.

It's always difficult to "act normal" at the best of times, but when the fluid in your body is mainly vodka and you are faced with an interrogation that could see you chucked back on the plane before they've had chance to suck the trumpy air out, it's just difficult to stand up straight.

I could feel the nervous anxiety get to me as I shuffled forward in the queue and as we got closer to the front I was really worried that as soon as I reach the desk I'll immediately crack like an egg and want to confess to anything and everything. I also started to recall how I'd mercilessly taken the mickey out of Donald Trump in the first book and started to worry just in case I'd been put on a US Homeland Security watch list.

Shit!

It's my turn... (try not to look like a murderer or a terrorist, stand up straight, don't breathe on him... just walk up to the desk and smile).

He stared right at me.

This was his first question:-

"Mr Hadley. Do you know where Lord Lucan is?"

Pathetic me: "**YES**!"

US Customs Guy: "And you do know where they buried Shergar?"

Pathetic me: "**YES!!**"

US Customs Guy: "Did you once dress up as a girl for a "laugh" with your mates and secretly keep the dress on for the weekend?"

Pathetic me, bawling: "**YES!!!** But it was sooo comfy... please don't tell me mum..."

I'd make a terrible spy.

Luckily he didn't ask me what *really* happened to Hammy the school hamster during the 1982 school holidays (a secret I will take with me to my grave. RIP Hammy and sorry again...) and it's a fingerprint test rather than a breathalyser test, so once I'd satisfied Officer Chad-Bill Buckley Jnr that I was no more a threat to US Homeland security than Spongebob Squarepants, we were allowed through the gate to retrieve our suitcases.

After what seemed like an age to get them (my cases are *always* the last to appear) we headed toward the exit to get the shuttle bus. After hours trapped inside the plane smelling other people's farts and the trauma of arrivals, I felt a huge sense of happiness and relief.

We were chatting away just as we saw the first signs and posters for Disney and Universal, a moment which led to Lottie and I having an excited hug and me getting a bit teary again as it dawned on me we were here.

Actually *here*.

In Florida.

Just me and my baby girl.

I'm filling up as I write this. It was a very special moment.

We trundled outside to be met by that first, fabulous blast of fresh, warm Florida air and we both smiled at the thought that we'd have this weather over the next week or so, instead of grey, bleak, miserable Dudley.

Enthused by the fact we were here and excited at the thought that it was still early enough to maybe get in to one of the parks, we loaded our stuff in to the shuttle bus and headed off to our posh digs.

Our choice of accommodation for this week's shenanigans is Mr Universal's Hard Rock hotel, a beautifully designed stack surrounded by swaying palm trees next to an alligator infested lake and only a short waddle through a snake-ridden park to Universal Studios. It's also handily placed to "City Walk", Universal's entertainment area that's jam packed with fab restaurants, cool bars, trendy shops and top notch nightly entertainment. A bit like Disney Springs on acid.

Funnily enough, the theme of the Hard Rock Hotel is rock music, and throughout the hotel there are loads of posters, statues and rock memorabilia with a musical vibe everywhere. Even the staff all dress as roadies, with bandanas, cool bracelets and funky hairdos.

The Hard Rock lobby is ace, with marble floors and a sweeping lounge area, dominated by a massive screen playing music videos. I knew I was going be at home here as soon as we arrived as they were playing 1980's videos, with "Never Gonna Give You Up" by Rick Astley on first, followed by "Wake Me Up Before You Go Go" by Wham.

Never one to miss an opportunity to embarrass my teenagers, I sang and bopped away to young George Michael as we checked in and went through the payment process. Lottie started to edge further away and was almost over the other side of the lobby as I started to do the two-step, arm swing sway to "Karma Chameleon" by Culture Club.

Great tune.

As it happens, this was also the moment when I reckon I was "spotted" for the first time. A couple and their teenage daughter were just behind me in the queue, and I recognised them from our plane. As I was singing and bopping away to Boy George, I noticed the young girl keep nudging her mum, pointing and laughing at me.

They never ACTUALLY came over to say hello but I'm dead sure they knew who I was – just the sight of me made them laugh!

Gotta count, right?

Ok, maybe not…

Check in completed by a young hipster called Billy-Bob Trey Hunter III, I grabbed our gear and sashayed over to find Lottie. Before we headed off to room 3149, we had a little look around to check out all the memorabilia and the Hard Rock gift shop.

It's all very impressive. Each piece of memorabilia pays homage to one of the big names – there's an outfit worn by Lady Gaga, a glittery suit that Elvis once wore in Vegas and a signed guitar from ACDC.

As we wandered round, I couldn't help but feel a sense of rising disappointment however, despite his decades of success, a worldwide fanbase and a string of massive hits, there is not one single mention of the greatest musical icon of them all – Barry Manilow.

I'm a big fan of Barry Manilow and must have seen him perform at least 30 times over the years. It stems from my mum – she was a fan as soon as Barry and his big nose burst on to the scene way back in the early 1980's, with his music filling our house on a daily basis. There was hardly a moment when the Hadley gramophone wasn't blasting out one of Bazza's finest vinyls and it became the soundtrack to my teenage years.

No wonder I'm a weak, emotional wreck.

Anyway, me and Bazza have been companions ever since and he's helped me through many a dark time and a broken heart. In my opinion, he's every bit as good as your Freddie Mercurys, your Madonnas or your John Lennons and I'm amazed there wasn't some tribute to him like a lock of his golden hair, a tour jacket or a picture of his nose.

Enough of complaining and back to the story. Lottie and I were keen to unpack and explore so we headed off down the long corridors for that exciting moment when you open the hotel room door for the first time and get sight of your digs for the week. Each room in the hotel has been themed with a nod to a musical icon or band, like *U2*, *Prince* or *Slade*.

So, planning ahead, a few weeks ago I rang The Hard Rock Hotel reservations to make sure Lottie and I got the Barry Manilow suite.

My request was ignored. Maybe it was a bad line or maybe Billy-Bob Trey Hunter III's mate just didn't understand my Black Country accent (Fancy not understanding me! Pah! For all he knew I could have been the great Noddy Holder himself!) so instead we've been put in the **Don Henley** room.

I have no idea who he is. Not a clue. I thought he was a snooker player, so when we got to room 3149 I was mildly disappointed when I found out he was actually a singer and I wouldn't be able to play a few frames.

Despite my disappointment, the Don Henley room was ace. A huge TV overlooking two massive double beds, a gigantic wardrobe and a nice bathroom. We had a nice view over the park so we could watch people being bitten by snakes and all around the room there were cool pictures along the rock and roll theme.

The Hard Rock is so cool you can actually order a guitar and amp on room service! Although they rejected my request for a ukele, thus denying Lottie and the rest of the hotel the chance to see my George Formby impression (I can't actually play the ukele, although I can do the funny voice. My musical talent extends only to the triangle, which I learned to play during my time in a Jamaican reggae band where I'd just dance and ting).

There's even a full-length mirror with a scale down the left, indicating the height of rock heroes past and present. I'm taller than Adele but not as tall as Bruce Springsteen unless I spike my hair up. And Lottie is as tall as Madonna and Pink! (For your information, Snoop Dogg was the tallest at 6 foot 4 while Shirley Temple was closer to the skirting board at 4 foot 2).

And I never knew Elton John was so short! I think they must have measured him while he was kneeling down...

Sadly, Barry Manilow was again overlooked on the mirror so I rectified this appalling oversight with a Sharpie (fyi he's exactly 6 foot in his cotton socks) and proceeded to write a disgruntled complaint letter to the manager here at Hard Rock about the shocking omission of one of the world's leading artistes in his supposed Hard Rock Hall of Fame.

After checking the loo for snakes and alligators, Lottie and I started to unpack our clothes, make up and face creams. To help us in our task, I put the telly on so I could get my fix of the brilliant American adverts and find out what new cures they have for piles.

I love these adverts. I love how every advert for any curing potion or medication has to have a disclaimer at the end stating it may <u>cause</u> the ailment it's aiming to cure! Genius!

"RHOID-BLAST! The no nonsense way to nuke those bum grapes!"

* lowers voice and talks dead fast **

"Do not swallow. Causes bad breath. Causes nostril hair growth. Side effects include nausea, vomiting and finding Mrs Brown's Boys funny. You may go blind. You may go bald. If you're already blind and bald, you may get piles. Or die"

The best advert of the day however was the one for Spam, which is seemingly having a renaissance over here in the States whilst in the UK it's mainly used as a substitute for dog food or fishing bait. They have catchy tag lines for the advert like:

"SPAM! Don't knock it til you've fried it!" and ***"S izzle P ork A nd Mmmmmm"***

Spam has definitely had a big re-brand over here and is somehow being sold as a health food. In one advert, it's pictured next to a pile of salad!

Who said Americans don't do irony.

You can buy Hot and Spicy Spam, Chorizo Spam, Smokey Bacon Spam and even Cheesey Spam. Which is all well and good except for one thing – it's still Spam. You can dress it up all you like, but it's still just salty, fatty mashed up bits of pig in a tin.

I'm gonna send this to Mr Spam, so he can use it as the next advert slogan.

"Spam - like putting lipstick on a pig"

Ironically, the Spam adverts did the trick and made both of us hungry so we abandoned the packing and braved the snake park in search of a Spam Teryaki burger over at City Walk. This proved to be a fruitless quest so instead we settled for a Voodoo Donut each (they're fab!) and a promise to eat a proper meal later at Bubba Gumps. There was still enough hours in the day for us to hit Universal Studios for a quick run around and in no time at all we had managed to have a go on our absolute fave, Rip Ride Rockit and the ace Jimmy Fallon In New York ride.

(Note to self - George at Asda cotton boxers aren't the wisest choice in 100 degree heat, unless you want your ballbag permanently splayed and stuck to the inside of your thighs like some sort of flying squirrel)

We ended our first day on a high, sitting side by side on stools at the bar in Bubba Gumps, eating delicious shrimp washed down with a few cocktails, going over the day's events and excitingly planning tomorrow's adventures. We absolutely love Bubba Gumps – the food is delicious, the staff are ace and there's Forrest Gump memorabilia throughout the restaurant. The film is played silently on a loop on all the TV's, and it's difficult not to just sit there, transfixed by Tom Hanks and mouthing every word yourself.

The boozey cocktails and the sad bits of the film started me off again, and I did get a little emotional as we sat there, me and my little girl together in our favourite place. Before we left, we got the barman, Troy-Dexter Arizona, to take a lovely picture of the two of us sitting there amongst a pile of shrimp shells to record the moment for posterity and with full bellies and tired legs, we headed back to the Don Henley room for some kip.

This had been a long but wonderful day – it started off many hours ago in The Black Country and ended in a hotel bedroom in Orlando, both of us falling immediately in to a deep sleep, getting much needed rest for the next day's adventures – more Universal and our first trip to see Barry Potter.

Mr Cody-Bob B. Alfonso Junior III
House Manager,
Universal Hard Rock Hotel
5800 Universal Blvd,
Orlando,
FL 32819, USA

2nd August 2018

Ref: Where's Barry?

Dear Mr Alfonso Junior III,

I hope you are well. I recently arrived at your hotel from Dudley in the UK. You might have heard of Dudley as it's where Noddy Holder comes from. You know, Noddy out of Slade? He's the one that does the singing and yelling and has got the big chops.

I like your hotel mate, it's very cool n that and all your "crew member" staff are really nice and helpful. The drinks are a bit pricey, mind.

Anyway, the reason I'm writing to you is this. I love all the music stuff and I love the way you have all the memorabilia from some of the biggest heroes in rock.

But I have to ask, why oh why is there no mention of Barry Manilow?

You have Pat Benatar, Bruce Springsteen and even Neil Diamond, but absolutely nothing to commemorate one of the biggest rock stars of all time!

I doh get it mate. Look, I'll accept he ay everyone's cup of chai latte with his rubbery face and big nose, but how can you possibly leave him out of your hotel showcase of musical talent **whilst still including Don Henley**?

And why is there never any of his music playing in the lobby? I even asked your lobby DJ, Vinyl Richie, and he said he didn't have any of Barry's tunes!

Look, I ay gonna make a fuss about it, but just send me a couple of cocktail vouchers and promise me you'll at least include "Copacabana" on the playlist for the next time I'm at the pool and you won't hear from me again.

Oh, and if you're stuck for memorabilia, it could be your lucky day! I just so happen to have my "***Barry - Live at Blenheim Palace"*** tour t-shirt with me from 1983! It's the special limited-edition pink one with the tassels and sequins. My mum brought it for me but I don't think she'll mind me selling it to you so long as it ends up in one of your big glass cases.

Shall we say $250.00?

Hope to hear from you soon, just shove a note under the door if you wanna meet up.

Yours,

Disgruntled of Dudley

Michael Hadley, room 3149

Day 2 - Barry Potter day

Today's look: *Black Country Boy*

Shirt - Jacamo, clearance
Shorts - JD Sports, Dudley
Trainers - £15, Lidl

Last year's blogging "trend" for recording the number of steps taken, calories consumed and dollars spent seems to have stopped (hope it's nothing to do with me relentlessly taking the mickey...) but thankfully I did find some comedy gold in one or two bloggers publishing what they wore each day. As I'm considered something of a trendsetter in The Black Country, and conscious of the fact that I'm bound to be spotted as some point by a fan, I bought a whole new wardrobe before heading out and I'm happy to share that with you here each day.

Ladies, if your husband needs a few fashion tips or you'd just like him to be a little more like me, feel free to get in touch.

Speaking of my non-celebrity status, I've managed to get through two busy airports packed with holiday Fams, check in to my hotel and wander around a theme park and have **still** yet to be recognised. I'm beginning to think it's because:

A) nobody knows, or cares, who I am and I've **hugely** overestimated my alleged "fame"

and

B) I just have one of those faces that's instantly forgettable. Pretty much all my life I've made a zero memorable impression on people I've met, whether it's at school, work or socially. I went to a school re-union once and was politely asked to leave as they thought I was a taxi driver. I've had follow up business meetings where I've had to remind the guy that he only met me a few weeks ago.

No-one ever seems to remember me.

Even my mum calls me mate.

Hoping for better luck today and a chance to win my bet with Lottie, we woke up early and after a quick shower followed by a grab and go breakfast from The Hard Rock Café, we jumped on to our Kwidditch sticks under the Harry Potter cloak of anonymity and flew off to Hogwarts for a poke around.

I don't want to alienate any of you here (especially all you moggles who love all this Harry Potter nonsense) but I really don't get it. I don't think I've ever managed to watch any of the films all the way through even though they seem to be on my television every bloody night. However, I confess I do get mildly interested when Hermeeownee comes on the screen, obviously now she's "grown up", if you know what I mean.

Don't get me wrong, I have a huge amount of admiration for Harry, especially as he pretty much gave up on being a normal teenager and chucked all his energy into making movies as soon as he found out he was a wizard.

I tell you something, if I found out that I was a wizard at 13 and had magic powers, I'm certain I wouldn't have been pissing about making films.

I'm fairly sure I'd have spent most of my time making myself invisible and magically transporting myself in to Mrs Baggot's house next door while she got undressed

Or the girls changing rooms at Dudley Comprehensive just after PE. That changing room, and the film Porkys, formed the basis of many of my fantasies as a young teen, and led to me spending an awfully long time alone in my bedroom.

And when I found my first ever copy of the Grattan catalogue, I became a virtual recluse. My mum didn't used to wash my bedsheets – she'd just chuck them over the line and knock them clean with a toffee hammer.

And I also admire the fact that it's based on a true story but surely you can only make ONE film? What is there, about 7?

Talk about stretching it out...

The other thing I don't get is why kids dress up in them big cloaks - it's 34 degrees man!

It's not even 10 o clock, the pavement has already burnt the soles off my Lidl trainers, my eyeballs are melting and my head's on fire, yet there's kids who have covered themselves head to toe in thick, black cloth so as they can stand in front of a pretend shop window waving a $40 plastic wand over and over again just to try to get something to twitch a few inches.

Good on yer Harry, me old son, you've well and truly cashed in as there wasn't a wobbly shop window, wishing well or poster that hadn't got a queue of hot sweaty kids waiting to swish an expensive piece of tat around while their mum loses her shit cos they're not standing in exactly the right spot.

"Fuh heaven's sake Bradley-Crystal Bethany, how many times do I gotta tell ya...? Keep freakin still!"

To be honest, this isn't a new phenomenon to me. There was a bloke in Dudley called Dirty Barry that used to dress in a long dark coat similar to Harrys, and he used to wave his wand into shop windows trying to get something to twitch a few extra inches too.

Usually dress shop windows though.

Until he got locked up.

"Arresto pervertum"

We needed to get out of the heat already and where better to do that than inside Harry's big plastic castle for a game of Kwidditch. As residents of Hard Rock, we get Universal Smug Passes included in the price of $300.00 a night, which entitles us to jump to the front of any queue in the two parks. It also entitles you to be a self-centred, arrogant, big headed twat as you skip past all the other hot, bored customers who haven't been fleeced in to staying at a so called "Rock" hotel where there's no mention of Barry Manilow.

I still can't get over that, can you tell?

We flashed our Smug Passes to the young lad dressed as a trainee wizard and before you can say *"Espresso Obligardum"* we were headed to the Kwidditch Transportation Boarding Area, ready to be chucked around for 5 minutes chasing Harry Potter. I declined the very kind offer of a Child Swap as I'm sort of happy with the one I've already got and to be honest most of the kids in the Swap Cave looked a bit grubby and high maintenance to me.

Game over and as if by magic our Kwidditch sticks dropped us off in Ye Olde Worlde Harry Potter Gift Shoppe. I did check to see if they'd answered my request for a woman's size Hermeeownee dressy up outfit as obviously Wifey needs a present. Kristie-Lou Pomagne Chantelle behind the till gave me a bit of a funny look which would suggest not, although I did notice a couple of other dads discreetly eavesdrop with interest. Maybe next time, lads. I'll keep checking and let you all know if it's a thing.

We wandered back down the hill and towards Wobbly Shop Street, and, noticing that there was hardly a queue for "Ollivanders Wand Shop", we headed over. For those that don't know (me included as I've just had to Google it), the Ollivander family make all the wands that are being swished in shop windows. It's really them, honest, and not a family from China called Wang.

Ollivanders Wand Shop is where you can Magically exchange around $30 for a basic entry level wand that doesn't "work". If you're extra gullible or if you have kids that have trouble pretending, you can pay a lot more for one.

See? Young Harry has got something for every pocket, bless him. That's the Magic of Harry Potter right th£r£.

Inside Ollivanders, you are treated to a 5 minute display where a failed English actor in a big long cloak pretends to be Garrick Ollivander himself and randomly chooses some kid from the crowd to use as a guinea pig for testing his wand.

Harry must be religious as I'm pretty sure the same thing has been going on for years in the Catholic church.

"Priestus Depravium!"

We lined up inside the shop and just as the door closed behind us the pretend Ollivander launched into his routine. Lottie was wearing a birthday badge given to her by one of the Hard Rock crew members, despite the fact that her birthday was 6 weeks ago, and dear old Ollivander must have clocked this as he only went and chose Lottie for a wand fitting!

"Freebie Magicko Wandus!"

This guy was dead good at pretending to be Ollivander and was both extremely convincing and very entertaining. All that money spent on getting into RADA hadn't been wasted after all. He held us all spell bound as he went over various options for the perfect wand for Lottie, making the kids giggle and performing magic tricks. I thought he was ace – not because of his performance but because we were going to get a free wand and secretly I wanted to see if I could use it to cast a sexy bedtime spell on Wifey when I got back.

"Smoochiatus Fornico!"

At the end of the performance, Lottie was ushered away in to a secret room with her new, specially selected wand and I followed excitedly behind, eager to see what we had won and how much it might be worth on Ebay.

Readers, all I can say here is this – that Harry Potter is a tight-fisted little git. The wand isn't free at all and the one that pretend Ollivander has "specially selected" for Lottie was $95.00! The cheeky sod.

"Bastardio Ripoffiosum!"

We pushed our way out of the door and past a line of frustrated kids in black cloaks, swatting wands and trying to make some lanterns light up and a thick looking kid waving his wand at a dustbin. We watched him nearly cack himself when the rubbish started to move and a squirrel jumped out.

They're little buggers ya know squirrels. I watched one rummage around in a pushchair once and actually open the lids of Tupperware container jars to fetch out the kiddies snacks! That's true, that is. Probably.

Back out in the sunshine, I experienced the absolute best part of the trip so far. Lottie and I just sat on the wall in the middle of Harry Potter Land, together on a beautiful Orlando day. All around us holiday mums pushed their beautiful kid's around, holiday dads moaned about the price of everything, and young, excited kids fulfilled their wildest dreams, pretending to be at Hogwarts.

All of this played out in front of us like a movie, the Wobbly Shops as the backdrop and all the holiday makers as the unwitting extras in our own comedy film. We sat for ages, people watching, drinking Butter Beer and acting daft. I made Lottie laugh with some terrible jokes and she begged me not to embarrass her (again).

It was heaven - just me and my beautiful daughter under the Florida sun, in a happy place, laughing, bonding and making memories that will last forever.

You can't buy that folks.

But if you could, Harry Potter would magically turn it into an "experience" and magically make $300 disappear off your credit card.

We slowly got ourselves together and after taking loads of great pictures to record the day for posterity, we shuffled over to the Hogwarts Express Train Station and a chance to escape the burning sun. I don't mind admitting this to you, dear reader, and this may come as a bit of a surprise seeing as I'm all butch n that, but I used to be a trainspotter. As a result, I get quite a nice warm feeling about being on or around trains - even the pretend one being operated by Harry Potter.

Ahhh, yes. The damp stench of an old platform, the rats running over the lines, the air of utter despair caused by decades of neglect... you can't beat a train station. Me and my spotty mates from Dudley used to spend all our weekends at train stations when I was a young teenager, wrapped up warm in our snorkel parkas and eating cheese and pickle sandwiches whilst writing down all the train numbers in a spiral bound notebook.

Whilst all the other lads at my school were doing daft things like having their first taste of booze and working out how to undo girls' bras with two fingers, me and my little gang used to travel all over the country spending our time looking at trains and learning how to be a sad loner on freezing cold platforms in places like Crewe, Walsall and Immingham.

No wonder I didn't have a girlfriend til I was 20.

The Harry Potter station and the train that magically transports you to the other park without actually moving is spot on and in no time at all we re-emerged in the bright sunshine, right next to Harry Potters Diagonal Alley.

This area is relatively new and built to cope with the ever increasing numbers of gullible muggles who have more money than sense and don't mind parting with $50.00 for a set of 4 Magical Harry Potter teaspoons.

In saying that, I actually like Diagonal Alley as it's well shaded, nice and cool and they have street entertainment in the form of some very pretty girl singers.

And because it reminds me a lot of Dudley.

Just like Dudley, it has hidden dark alleys for the muggers, badly cobbled streets cos the council have got no money to fix them and a load of useless old shops selling tat. And, just like Dudley, most of the shops are on the skunt due to subsistence from the old mine shafts.

Oh, oh, oh...**and** we have a dragon! Although she's slumped *outside* the bank rather than on it and every so often breathes vomit instead of fire.

If only there were a Vape Shop and a Mr Chicken, it'd be spot on.

There is another similarity that makes me think Jay K Rowley based Diagonal

Alley on Dudley. There was a big family who lived on the estate near me called the Gringotts. They were a fearsome family and there must have been about 20 of 'em, all short and stocky and bred to steal and fight. Even the women.

Just like the Jay K Rowley "Gringott" the dad was ugly, fat and bald and he used to work in a bank too. Well, I say "work"... I mean rob but it's almost the same. Especially in Dudley.

Lottie and I ate in a medieval banquet hall called The Leaky Cauldron and went through the usual routine of getting a few mouthfuls in to a meal before she had to put her headphones in to block out the noise of my choffing. To be fair, I did order BBQ chicken wings. She'd have been better off wearing a deep-sea diver's mask.

We wobbled over the bridge and meandered toward Springfield, home of the ace Simpsons ride and even acer Duff Beer stand. We sat on a wall and chatted as I supped on a Duff (not a euphemism) and did some more people watching.

We hung around for a while until the storm clouds came growling over, so decided to make a dash for the new "Fast and Furious" ride before we got soaked.

Man alive, what a waste of time that ride is!

Fast and Furious? More like Slow and Stodgy. My first Mini Metro went faster than that ride.

We were both pretty knackered by now so agreed to call it a day for theme park based fun and headed back to the hotel and see if Mr Hard Rock had replied to my Disgruntled of Dudley letter.

He hadn't.

Lottie face-timed the dog which totally freaked her out (Molly the Cockapoo, not Lottie) and I watched some more bonkers US television for a chance to see what mischief my old mate Donald Trumpet has got in to today. I'll say one thing, it's never dull with that big dullard being the most powerful man in the world is it?

I reckon he's got a big spinning wheel in the Oval Office, a bit like that one on "Wheel Of Fortune", and each category has got either an ethnic minority, a specific religion or a downtrodden social group written on it in **big** letters so he can read it. When he's done discharging the fire extinguisher sized can of hairspray on to his wig, he spins the Wheel of Persecution and whichever group it lands on, it's their turn for abuse today.

"We're gonna build a wall, the greatest wall, I build the greatest walls EH-VERRR, everybody knows that, and we're gonna do it right here in Washington".

"Yeah, we gotta address the problem, and it really is the biggliest of problems lemme tell ya. There is no bigglier threat to the security of our nation right now than the one we face from these..."

** pauses to spin wheel **

"One-Legged Transgender Albino Mongolian Goat Herders...".

Personally, I think anyone who can't be trusted with his own hairspray shouldn't be in charge of the nuclear button.

After a bite to eat in a lovely Italian restaurant and a shufty around City walk, the comfort of our fabulous beds in Don Henley Room 3149 was calling. Before I collapsed exhausted in to bed, I had just enough time to check that all the walking I've done today hasn't seen me shrink below Frank Sinatra in the celeb mirror. Thankfully, it hadn't, and I was still just below Mariah Carey. Ooooh...

I bid my beautiful daughter goodnight and thanked her for sharing a wonderful day with me, then tried to get to sleep quickly so I didn't miss the start of my dream. Tonight's should be a good one...

** closes eyes and crosses fingers **

"Please let it be about Hermeeownee,

Please let it be about Hermeeownee,

Please let it be about Hermeeownee ..."

Day 3 - Chillin and more Universal

Today's look: *Charity Chic*

T Shirt - Army and Navy Stores, West Bromwich
Shorts - Dudley Dog Rescue
Trainers - Aldi middle aisle

I reached the big half century this year so I'm at that age where fashion sense and clothes that fit properly is mostly a distant memory and an outfit that matches and looks good a mere aspiration. Most days I look like I've got dressed in a rushed panic in a pitch black room.

The "T shirt from the Army and Navy Stores" line above is actually true though – there was a time when my mum and dad really were really struggling financially (my mum was down to just 3 fur coats at one stage) so to save money and make sure that the weekly food budget could stretch to that fourth bottle of Bells for me dad, my mum used to buy me and my sister quite a lot of clothes from there.

It's not much fun going to school in Dudley dressed as a Japanese Admiral.

Or when your sister's dressed as a German Stormtrooper.

Before I regale you with stories from today's adventure, here's a quick update on my non-celebrity status:

Nothing. Zilch. Naff all.

Zero sightings so far. Although, yesterday someone excitedly posted on Facebook that they'd "spotted" me in a park I wasn't even in. It must have been some other portly yet ruggedly handsome stud muffin I suppose.

Today's plan was for Lottie and me to chill by the pool in the morning then head out for a bop round one of the Universal parks in the afternoon.

This is for two reasons – we had a full-on day yesterday and decided we needed a recharge, and because the first few signs of strain between us have appeared. It's only been a few days but already she's started to crack as my chewing's seemingly got louder, I'm constantly in her way and apparently I'm always on my phone (ironic coming from a teenager, uh?) so we decided to relax for a bit with our headphones in so we don't have to look at or talk to each other.

Paying about $300.00 a night at the Hard Rock hotel still isn't quite enough to get you a breakfast each day, so part of my morning ritual has been a trip downstairs to the Convenient But Terribly Expensive Marketplace Shop to get some fodder. It's a small, weirdly V-shaped room situated on the ground floor of the hotel and is part shop / part fast food / part café.

And absolutely bloody freezing.

The pool is only 20 yards from the shop door and out there you've got people wearing bikinis and swimming trunks and **still** sweating their tits off cos it's hotter than Satan's ballbag, yet inside the shop the staff have got their thermals on because the aircon has been set to "Arctic Tundra".

You get a full-on, icy blast as soon as you walk in, your nipples stick up like lorry wheel nuts and your willy disappears. It's like you've been Frozoned.

I shivered around the shop this morning and grabbed a few bits for me and Lot to have in the room. She had a low-fat yogurt and some fruit and I'm on a diet so just had a sausage, bacon and egg bagel with extra cheese. And a donut.

The girl behind the till, Marlie-Jayne Tramadol, struggled to give me my change back as it's difficult to move in an eskimo suit, so I left it as a tip and headed up to room 3149, making it back just as my nipples defrosted.

Lottie groaned when she could see what I'd got for breakfast, so anticipating another whinge about my chobbling, I retired to the bathroom and ate my bagel sitting on the bog with a bath towel over my head.

A few satisfying burps and cheeky trumps heralded the end of breakfast, so we chucked some bits together and headed down to the pool before I could feel the carb rush come on and needed a power nap. Well, it was almost 10 o clock.

We grabbed a couple of big, fluffy towels, picked out two sunbeds in a quiet place away from any noisy kids and lay down under the hot sun.

It was absolutely fanbloodytastic.

For a few hours, Lottie bopped away on her sunbed listening to soul music and I snoozed, drank cocktails and listened to more Barry Manilow. Heaven.

The Hard Rock pool area is really nice – crystal clear water surrounded by massive palm trees, a great bar area and enough room for you to find a bit of private space if you're a bit of a fatty and don't want anyone to see your stretch marks.

When it got too hot, Lottie would nudge me and for 10 minutes or so we'd go and sit in the pool together, lapping up the water to cool us down and chat shit. We're dead good at that, me and my girl. We have made up, nonsensical conversations about anything and everything, both of us trying to keep a straight face and battling hard not to giggle.

When she was about 8, Lottie and I invented an entirely new language which we called **Shabibban**. We'd talk for ages in our made-up language, very often in public, and it sounded sort of Arabic mixed with Russian, with a tiny bit of Dutch and lots of exaggerated, Italian style hand gestures. It would drive Wifey mad as we'd pretend to be talking about her in Shabibban, occasionally stopping the conversation to point at her and burst out laughing.

Not sure how we got away with that bit, actually.

I really soaked up that moment. I have a perfect picture of it in my mind's eye – a cloudless, bright blue sky, cool music in the background and me and Lottie acting daft in the pool. As the palm trees swayed, the water lapped up over my muffin tops and the whiff of Hawaiian Tropic filled my nostrils, I remember turning to her and saying that she should try to remember it too. And that moments like these are the reasons why I work so hard.

Us Grumpy Dads can be really hard work, tell the worst jokes, make annoying noises when we eat and sometimes be too wrapped up in our own world and workload to really see what's really important that's going on around us, but deep down all we want to do is love, protect and provide for our Fam.

And at that moment, I'm proud to say that I'd done exactly that.

We had a tasty lunch right next to the pool as the DJ ramped up the holiday toons. We were both in high spirits and funked out to some Stevie Wonder as I got totally mullered on margaritas - is it me or are American measures mahoosive? No wonder I always look pie eyed on all the holiday photos.

I was absolutely plastered exhausted, so as Lottie went off to the room to get ready, I had another power nap (fourth one today and it's only 2 o clock!) I woke up groggily a little while later to see a message to say she'd gone in to the park ahead of me, so I got my drunken ass in to gear and headed back to the room for another power nap.

I'm kidding. Although I did have a little lie on the bed.

There are worse ways to spend a Saturday, I can tell you.

Anyway, done chillin' for a while so early evening / late afternoon I headed off to Isles of Adventure to catch up with my girl. We had a good wander round, did a bit of tat browsing and then headed off to one of our absolute favourite rides, "Kong, Skull Island". This is a simply superb ride and if you're ever there, go and do it. You will not be disappointed. Especially if you like to stand in a dark, dank queue for 2 hours just to spend 5 minutes being scared to death by vomiting tape worms, giant cockroaches, man eating dinosaurs and a 100 foot, angry chimp.

I was feeling a little peckish as we hadn't eaten for three hours, so I called it time for tea. Luckily, Kong is right next door to some sort of Western Smokehouse that smelled amazing, so in we waddled for some good 'ole fashioned Humerican food.

After what seemed like an age standing in a cafeteria style queue, we found ourselves up next to be served. Casey-Lou Joleen behind the counter totally misunderstood my accent and proper got the hump when I asked for a spitroast so instead her manager, Krystal-Meth Angelica, served me a plate of ribs, fries and a side of corn on the cob.

Readers, there is nothing more horrific than watching a flabby middle-aged man devour ribs and a buttery corn cob. We should be forced to eat it in the dark or behind a screen.

When I eat corn on the cob it's like a tree surgeon shredding logs into one of them funny looking machines on the back of a pick-up, with bits flying anywhere and everywhere – even occasionally in my mouth.

And the ribs! Wowzer. I was like a caveman, devouring the tasty meat off the brittle bone, sucking up the juice and licking my fingers clean with a happy, satisfied burp.

Lovely stuff.

I looked up to realise Lottie had moved tables and with one final lick of my lips and a check to make sure that I'd not left any tasty bits of cartilage, I went off to get her and we headed off to The Hulk.

One of many unfortunate side effects of getting old is that more food gets stuck in your teeth. This never used to happen before I hit 45, I'm sure. The tooth gap thing sort of started the same time as the involuntary noises when I bend down, or the one, rogue thick, black hair that grows suddenly and protrudes off the top of my ear like a planted flag on Everest.

Any kind of meat is a challenge with gappy teeth and ribs are definitely top of the list for getting deeply wedged in. I've learned to carry a few toothpicks with me for such an occasion, so as we walked along in the dark I tried to tease out a nice chunk of rib that had got trapped in my lower molar.

Just as I dislodged it, a kid bumped into me causing the toothpick to break off in my gum. I then had to get another toothpick to get the first toothpick out. By the time we reached the Hulk, I'd managed to hoik them both out, leaving me looking like some sort of Hannibal Lector lookalike with meat round my chops and blood dribbling down my stubble.

Lottie went and shoved our loose items in the free lockers as I went off to the bog to wipe my face clean as I was scaring little kids. We then spent a short time queuing up for the Hulk ride, followed by an even shorter time being turned upside down and bumped from side to side whilst examining my own bumhole. I'm not a big fan of roller coasters as they mess my hair up, but at least tonight my underpants learned what colour fear is.

Lottie and I mooched around City Walk for a little while, people watching and chilling out to the live band. Eventually, we called it a day and headed back to the hotel, following other tired Fams on a stroll through Snake-Ridden Park.

We deliberately hung back from one Fam – they had three kids and a huge pushchair, completely loaded down with tat, and the mum had a bit of a limp - if the snakes were gonna bite, they'd have her first as she'd have struggled to run away.

The end of another wonderful day. I walked happily and proudly back to the room with my beautiful daughter, chatting away about our next adventure - we're off to Seaworld tomorrow to do some whale spotting.

Day 4 – Whale of a time at Seaworld

Today's look: *Cheekily Aquatic*

Shirt - Big and Tall Men
Shorts - Hand me downs
Hair - By L'Oreal, cos I'm worth it

Today started the same as the last few days - I woke up before Lottie and while she snored away I managed to drag my old, knackered body through a routine of trumps, joint cracks, moans and groans to psych myself up to using the in-room boiling contraption.

Neither kettle nor coffee machine, this thing is an abnormally large piece of kit that in contrast to its size delivers a ridiculously small hot water portion in return for huge amounts of human effort. Namely mine.

In other words, it's a pile of tinny, American cack.

It's about the size of one of those posh 4 slice toasters you'd pay £200 for in John Lewis and is ridiculously hard to operate, especially as I only want hot water to make tea (I always take my own Yorkshire Tea bags on holiday. Always)

You kick off the boiling process by pressing down hard down on one big button on the top, which in turn releases a coffee pod shaped trapdoor. I'm not making coffee so you have to close this firmly in order to open the water tank part at the back which jumps up like Arkwright's till. You then have to fill the water tank, snap the lid back shut and work out which button just does "boil".

There isn't one, but there is a row of cup shape buttons and a steam symbol, none of which boil water.

After angrily pressing every button, you eventually unlock the magic combination, the machine shrugs its metal shoulders and lets out a disgruntled, hissy sigh and spends the next five minutes grumpily chugging away like an old generator. Eventually, a thin, pathetic stream of tepid water dribbles out in to your cup as all the time it makes totally exaggerated gurgly steam noises.

All this for an amount of warm water that just about covers the mighty Yorkshire Tea bag.

The machine then let's out one huge, exhausted sigh and falls back to sleep, refusing to be ready for another ten minutes or until it's cooled down. It takes about 20 minutes to make two cups of tea, which is about as long as it's taken me to write about it, so I could of had 2 cups by now.

So instead of moaning about my lack of tea, let me tell you about our day in Seaworld.

I love Seaworld. You otter know that you always have a whale of a time here, I just dolphin(k) there's a better park. If you haven't already been don't be koi or mullet over, just flamingo! Even if you don't like fish, go for the halibut. It's only about sick squid to get in and Salmon Lottie had a great time here. We're dabb hands at it now, but if you can think of a better sea life park, let minnow.

Cod almighty these jokes are bad. I'll scale it back. Sorry, I'm doing it on porpoise.

They've updated Seaworld since our last visit and it's good to see how they continue with their amazing conservation efforts. I love how they get in to the real spirit of the ocean and name all the attractions after sea life – "Mako" the new rollercoaster, "Dolphin Cove" and "Stingray Lagoon".

New additions include Dr Kipper's Crab Clinic where they carry out extensive research into fish related reproductive diseases and Muff Cove, where for a small fee you can practise your diving skills.

Even the toilets have been given a makeover although it's a little confusing for first time visitors. Women have to just follow the signs for Tenalady Drips and fellas need to look out for the sign of the Turtles Head.

Me and my little fry Lottie had a great time, swimming along in the current of happy Fams like two happy fishes, sploshing from one amazing show to another, diving on to roller coasters and gawping like Dory at the amazing sea life in tanks.

We watched the dolphin show which was utterly fab. I have a soft spot for dolphins as they remind me of my time when I used to be involved with S.O.D.D's, the Society of Dudley Dolphins. We used to meet up every fortnight to discuss our love for anything dolphin related, but I left when they took in a load of new members from West Bromwich and it got a bit clicky.

In between cold drinks and looking at weird fish in tanks, we sat together and watched the daft sealion show and dared each other to go on every terrifying roller coaster. It was all fantastic.

The highlight of the entire day though was the One Ocean show, not just because of the amazing theatre in front of you in the shape of the awesome whales and the amazing tricks that they perform, but also because of the heart-warming tributes paid to members of the military past and present before the show starts. That's a real tear jerker for me, especially when you see the old guys stand up.

I also picked up a tip from this show which I've since incorporated into my daily work. In order to keep the whales in tow and carry on performing their stupendous tricks, the trainers have strategically placed buckets filled full of dead fish to chuck in to the whale's mouth. It guarantees peak performance from the whale and acts as a treat when they've done a good job. I've now added the same thing in to my factory in Brierley Hill, with strategically placed buckets full of scratchings. Whenever one of my guys does something good, I go over to the bucket and grab a handful of the Black Country's favourite crunchy snack and feed them as they excitedly stamp up and down in happy anticipation. I did the same in the sales office but they're a bit more porky in there so used donuts instead. Productivity and sales are on the up!

At the end of the show I joined a queue of people waiting to say hi to some of the trainers down at the front. I was in such high spirits I excitedly told them how awesome they were and how much I enjoyed the show, much to Lottie's disgust. And, forever chivalrous, just as we were walking away I did my bit by helping to guide an excited blind lesbian away from one of the empty fish buckets.

Never let it be said that I don't do my bit to help out.

Being here with Lottie on a day like this is just the best feeling I could have as a person *and* as a Dad. One minute it's like being with my best mate, laughing and joking and playing up in a wonderful theme park and the next minute she's instantly back to being my little girl again, and I just want to love and take care of her and make sure she's having the best time.

Before we came away, I had a stern word with myself to throw off this invisible, grumpy cloak that all Dads seem to wear every day. You know, that invisible cloak that only The Fam have the ability to see that us Grumpy Dads have no idea that we're even wearing it. I vowed I'd chuck myself in to anything and everything and not let her down - not leave anything out here and have no regrets. That I'd really let myself go and push the limits of my physical and mental endurance.

And that's how I came to have Nemo painted on my face.

We strolled past the face painting stall and for a laugh I said "Ooooh, we should have our faces painted!", not thinking for a second that she'd say yes.

Quick as a flash, Lottie's all over it like a tramp on chips so asks the assistant, Brandy-Phoenix Arizona-Amber how much it costs to paint a fish on a fat man's face. It turns out she wasn't the actual face painter so she took a step back and shouted in to the Seaworld tat shop behind her:

"Gracie-Lou Mandy-Bailey-Amy Jane! Get yerself out here girl, we got ourselves a customer!"

Taking it as an insult that she's called for back-up in the form of *six* face painters for my chubby chops (maybe one for each chin?) imagine my surprise when Gracie-Lou Mandy-Mary-Amy Jane turns out to be just one little poppet of a girl.

She was dead sweet too. Cute as a button with a soft squeaky voice just like my precious Holly Willoughby, she gently dabbed my face with funny paint as I tried hard not to breathe 3 days' worth of booze on her and just a few minutes later Nemo magically appeared through a layer of factor 50 and five days of stubble, followed not long later by a beautiful pretty blue flower on Lottie's already beautiful face.

I half-jokingly asked if she was a real painter and did foreigners as my downstairs toilet could do with a lick but I don't think she heard me. Although as I handed over the $50, she did promise free touch ups all day.

Which was nice.

And so, Lottie and I finished our wonderful day at Seaworld with a slow walk to see the manatees and then shared a tub of Dippin' Dots, all the time being smiled at by passers-by as we strolled, as they obviously found it funny to see a middle aged man with Nemo painted on his face.

I loved it. It was a daft but not insignificant sign of the bond that we share and proof that I've well and truly shook off the Grumpy Dad cloak.

We arrived back at Hard Rock and we were met by a banging DJ playing some hot summer tunes as walked in to the lobby. We hung around for a while as this guy was really good, mixing it up and timing his sounds with a massive big video screen behind him. The music must have been too loud even for him though as he couldn't hear me when I asked for Copacabana by Barry Manilow.

We called it a day after a sharing platter of Mexican food at City Walk and went to bed happy, ready for a good night's sleep before tomorrow's blartfest – Toy Story Land.

Day 5 – A blartfest at Hollywood Studios

Today's Outfit: Classic sweatfeast

Shirt - TK Maxx jumble rail
Shorts - Borrowed from my cousin, Chubby Doug
Socks - West Bromwich indoor market

I've given up on the in-room tepid water dribbler masquerading as a coffee machine and instead went downstairs to brave the cold and get a coffee from the Convenient But Terribly Expensive Marketplace shop. Along with a range of super calorific breakfast items such as cheesy bacon croissants, donuts and bagels with peanut butter and jam, they offer a range of Starbucks blends where just one cup is the same price as a full English at Asda in Dudley.

With my hands full of stolen sachets of peanut butter and ranch dressing and my croissant tucked under my chin, I perused the coffee urns to decide which would most likely give me the quick buzz I needed to face the busy day ahead.

Veranda blend - Mellow and soft
Pike Place - Smooth and balanced
Cafe Verona - Roasty sweet with dark cocoa

None of them really appealed, so I asked the shivering girl behind the till, Poppy-Lou Champagne, if they had my favourite blend, **Dudley Dribble** - bitter, unbalanced with a hint of faggot.

She said she didn't know so she went and asked the guy serving the $10 croissants, Billy-Bob Hunter-James Jr III, but he was new to the job so wasn't sure either.

She asked the entire back room team but none of Trey, Scooter, Chip, Biff and Todd could help.

In the end I went for a *Fluff Paradise* - a soft mellow brew with chocolate, cinnamon, marshmallows and whipped cream, topped off with melted butter and sprinkles. I have been good and I'm watching my calorie intake so I mixed it with Half and Half instead of full fat cream (I used to go to school with a half and half, a very confused young person especially when it came to changing for PE)

With breakfast booty sorted I headed back to the room to thaw out and wake up my little nugget. Even though she's 18, Lottie still sleeps like a toddler and each morning I've woken up so far she's been in a different position in a different part of her bed. She's been half in / half out, diagonally across the bed, upside down, hanging off the side with her head near the carpet... as I walked in the room I half expected her to be asleep standing up.

As it happened, she was curled up in a snuggly ball so I gave her a little nudge and a kiss on the top of her head, then lay on my bed to drink my coffee before the whipped cream melted. At that point, I managed to break my previous personal record of annoying her as she moaned at me for gulping my coffee before she'd even opened her eyes.

I reckon her and Wifey got together before we left so Wifey could brief her on all the things to expect to be annoyed about. I bet she's got a long list of my annoying habits to look out for and on a daily basis Mummy's Little Envoy confers with Wifey in a game of Annoying Dad Bingo.

"Loud chewing? **Check**"
"Walking too slow?" **Check**"
"Dad dancing? **Check**"
"Saying inappropriate things to pretty waitresses? **Check**"

"House!!!"

Anyhow, she eventually roused and we both sat up in bed, eating breakfast with the TV volume on full blast so she couldn't hear me slurping on a croissant and when we were done started to get excited about the day ahead. This was the day we've probably both been looking forward to the most - our first of only two days this trip at one of Mr Disney's Psycho Parks, Hollywood Studios.

Like most Fams with little sproglets, films offer an incredible way to remember your kids growing up. Each one holds a special place in yours and your child's heart, and whether you sit and watch with them cuddled up on the sofa or they watch them alone, dancing and re-enacting it in front of the telly, they become a story in themselves about your life and the happy times spent watching them grow up. Every character, jokey catchphrase or song has a special meaning, unique to you or them.

Each film also benchmarks a different stage in their young lives, a bit like how songs become the soundtrack to your adult life. I only have to hear a few bars of certain songs from my youth to immediately feel like a teenager, or the sound of a romantic tune to remind me of how Wifey and I first fell in love. It's all Barry Manilow, obviously, but you get my point.

The Hadley storybook that played out in the background as Sam and Lottie grew up is Pixar.

Just those five letters make me want to cry. In fact, when we came to Hollywood Studios for the first time, they did exactly that. We turned the corner and saw the big "PIXAR" sign and both Wifey and I almost collapsed in a blubbering mess on the floor.

Each fabulous, beautiful Pixar production represents a different chapter as they went from cute sproglets to mardy teenagers and each one of the bittersweet songs provided a soundtrack to family life and times as we have watched them grow up. Sam is Toy Story through and through and it was played over and over again in our house. Totally coincidentally, Toy Story 3 was released on almost the exact same day in 2010 that Sam left primary school, so the scene with Andy going off to college and giving his toys to Bonnie had me and Wifey bubble snot crying in to our popcorn.

Lottie is Finding Nemo and she was just 5 when it was released. It's quite remarkable how Lottie has gone on to match the character of little Nemo – dogged, determined, single minded and prepared to fight for everything. The story line matches her life too, how we nearly lost her when she was really little, how we had to battle against all odds to keep her alive and how happy and thankful we are now we're all together.

With this in mind, I know I'm going to cry when I take my little Nemo to the new Toy Story Land for the first time.

And I did. Like a baby. It was a total blartfest.

And got added to the list of annoying things Dad does.

"Starts to cry and tries to hug me as soon as he sees Mr Potato Head? **Check**".

I cried all the way round as Lottie grew even more disgusted with me and warned me she'd go off alone if I didn't stop embarrassing her and taking pictures. I managed to compose myself by standing in a two-and-a-half-hour hot queue for the new Slinky Dog ride. Yes, there's nothing better to snap you back in to hot reality than sweating your cobs off, bored stiff while you shuffle along waiting for your turn. It was torture.

All that just to ride a dog. It'd take just twenty minutes or two WKD's in West Bromwich Wetherspoons.

We did the other rides, Alien Encounters and Toy Story Mania, and spent a while just strolling round, taking it all in. The place is well designed and there's interesting stuff and photo opportunities everywhere, There's loads of character meet and greets too and you can tell when Woody's turned up as there's a mad rush to get to the front of the queue - a bit like when it's packed at Aldi and they open a new till.

For me, the highlight of Toy Story Land was undoubtedly the Green Soldiers who are utterly brilliant. Not only do they look incredible, but they are genuinely funny, chatting away with the crowd and acting daft. They play silly games, dance and stick around for ages having their photos taken with adoring kids.

It really was a wonderful morning, but the rest of the park was calling and I'd decided to eat elsewhere as I didn't fancy the thought of chowing down on Woody's Lunchbox.

So I spent hours and hours having great fun with my little Nemo and we managed to do everything in the entire park - every ride and every show. I cried as often as Lottie let me. She allowed me to sniffle during the Beauty and The Beast stage show and blart like a baby when we sang "Let It Go" in Singalonga Frozen. I didn't cry but I found myself in a sweet moment and became totally overcome with love and emotion during The Little Mermaid, all the time with Lottie looking at me in disgust and telling me to not to "make it all weird as usual".

Continuing the theme of my Z celebrity status, absolute no-one spotted me today – I've come to realise that I'm about as popular as a trump in a wet suit.

Today was also our first experience of huge, and I mean huge, volumes of people, an increasingly annoying phenomenon which does seem to have got a whole load worse in recent years in Disney parks.

Warning - Grumpy rant on the way.

Is it me or are some people so stupid that they don't know how to walk straight? I mean, come on folks it ay difficult to simply walk in a straight line from the point you started from to the point you wanna get to somewhere in the distance.

What's with the meandering? I don't get it. So many times today we'd see someone come toddling towards us then inexplicably change direction to cut across our path, completely knocking you off and out of our stride.

Or, and this is even worse, some dopey idiot who's walking in front of you inexplicably and without warning coming to a sudden dead stop in front of you, causing you to stumble and spill your souvenir Let It Go Lemonade Slushy.

And, oh my god...

Oh. My. God!

** puts chubby hands to handsome Grumpy head in exasperation **

PUSHCHAIRS!!!

When did it become a thing that pushchairs had to be the size of a gypsy caravan?

When did they start selling buggies that have the extra big wheels, extended undercarriages with added storage trays, built in fans, sun shades and really long handle bars to hang more souvenir tat on?

And why does the pushing parent always get an urge to go suddenly and instantly sideways across a crowd?

Busy restaurants are the worst. So many times I've seen a bad tempered Military Mum use the pushchair as an excuse / battering ram just to blast her way in to or out of a busy restaurant, bosting people's ankles up, knocking tables over and generally causing mayhem as she stubbornly tries to manoeuvre a buggy the size of small potting shed on wheels through a two foot gap, all the while saying "Sorry! SoRREEE...!"

She's not sorry at all. That's just venting that is - the cry of a frustrated mum that's been saddled with the frustrating responsibility of pushing the buggy, knowing that everyone is looking at her with judgy eyes...

The size of these things is getting ridiculous though – surely no baby or toddler ever needs <u>that</u> much stuff. You're going for a day in a theme park, not on an expedition in search of a lost tribe in a Brazilian jungle.

We were getting ready to watch the parade here last time and just as it approached the crowds were being shooed out of the way. One posh stroller being hurriedly pushed by a Military Mum was packed to the hilt with Disney tat – it was so big and brightly lit with plasticky, annoying neon, pieces of crap it ended up in Mr Disney's parade by accident.

The mum and her entire family got sandwiched in between Moana's float and a gang of camp, body popping Stormtroopers.

Completely trapped, they decided to go with the flow so just styled it out, the dad shuffling along with his best snake-hipped, helicopter pilot dance while the kids flossed and the mum did the conga behind her caravan sized stroller all the way down Hollywood Boulevard.

I can feel another Disgruntled of Dudley letter coming on. I'm gonna write to Mr Disney and suggest he limits the number of kids allowed in and bans strollers altogether. Or make it so you pay by size... ooh that's a good idea, he could make loads of money from that cos I bet he's short of a bob or two.

We ended the day with a stroll down memory lane by catching a boat through alligator infested waters and headed off to The Beach Club (aka Mr Disney's Retirement Home for the Financially Retarded). I'm happy to report that since we stayed here last year it hasn't changed one bit. The smell of cabbage and wee pervades the air while rich Americans spend $300 on a steak. Lovely stuff.

Lottie and I sat in The Beach Club lobby and waited a while to get a caricature of the two of us together – the evidence of which is in your hand (unless you're reading a Kindle). Happy with the result, we headed out in to the warm Florida night and took our time wandering around The Boardwalk, eventually settling for some scoff at the ESPN Sports Bar. Lottie had a healthy chicken salad and I had the biggest burger I have ever seen in my life – I am trying to watch what I eat so I asked them to leave the tomato out. And swapped that for extra cheese, which seems about right in terms of calories.

We jumped in a cab back to Hard Rock and made it back just in time for a $15.00 gin and tonic (me, obviously) in the mega posh hotel bar. Lottie was pooped so headed off to bed as I sat like a lonesome cowboy in the bar and watched a young, handsome guy in a Stetson and tight jeans sing some good ole country and western tunes about his dog running off and catching his missus in bed with his dad.

Then went to bed depressed.

*****

Mr Walt Disney
The Big Castle
Magic Kingdom Theme Park
1180 Seven Seas Drive
Lake Buena Vista
Orlando,
FL 32830, USA

6th August 2018

Ref: Too many kids!

Dear Mr Disney,

I hope you are well. I hope this is the right address to write to – I'm guessing that it is as I'm sure I've seen you popping your head out of the castle during the fireworks display. To be fair, if I'd spunked all my days takings on some fireworks, I'd want to look as well so I don't blame you aer kid.

Listen, I've had an idea that I reckon could be good for you and if you like it I don't mind if you use so long as you give me an upfront payment.

I was in one of your other parks today – Hollywood Studios. I gotta tell ya, it's great n all that but hot diggety dawg it's busy! You could barely walk in a straight line without some twerp bumping in to ya,

And kids… god there were so many kids. They were bloody everywhere, swishing away with their light savers, shooting at each other with pretend cowboy guns or dressing up like a princess pretending to be Elsa out of Freezing. And there were some girls too.

Trouble is with kids they come with loads of baggage, if you know what I mean, both emotionally and physically. I'm talking about pushchairs here, Mr Disney. Some of these pushchairs are massive and I can't see that some of these parents actually need all that gear they bring in. And they cause total chaos too, always nipping your ankles or blocking exits.

So these are my ideas. You'll like this…

1) Limit the number of children any one family can bring in to the park.
2) Charge an entrance fee for pushchairs.

With the children idea, you could put a cap of say two kids per mum and dad (or mum / mum, dad / dad – need to be PC don't we, especially for the fudge packers and bean flickers as they get offended *really* easily). Parents will have to choose their least favourite child and for just a small fee they get left in a locked pen, like the ones they have at IKEA. You could charge extra for supervision, extra for food and extra again to watch TV!

If the parents don't like the thought of the kids locked up in a pen all day, they can come back at any time and pay again to swap him or her (or "it" if they're transgender – don't want to upset any of the He-She kids either) for any one of their other children.

For the pushchairs, I reckon you can introduce fees based on a simple size chart. For example:

Buggy / Puschair Type	Daily Price $
Single collapsibles	$5.00
Double, two storey collapsibles	$10.00
Triple, two storey contraptions with the big net luggage holdall at the bottom	$15.00
Those pull along wooden trucks that look like they've been used on a farm for turnip picking	$20.00

Buggy boards, large stick on visors, fans etc	$5.00 supplement per item
Anything over 3 foot wide or 4 foot long (proof of child required and not just an excuse to carry extra shopping and smuggle in wine)	Price on application

Just think of the money you can make from this Mr Disney! You can spend it all on more / better fireworks!

Look, I know you have far more cleverer people than me giving you marketing advice and of course you will have to check the legality of leaving the kids locked up all day, so I'll just leave the idea with you and you can just send me a fair payment.

Shall we say $250.00? Oh, and free park tickets for life. Oh, and Fast Passes for Flight of The Pandora too.

Hope to hear from you soon.

Yours, Disgruntled of Dudley,

Michael Hadley,

Room 3149, Hard Rock Hotel.

Day 6 – An airboat ride, plastic alligators and a meet up

Today's look: *Poncey Adventurer*

Nails – Cute Tickle Nails, Kissimmee
Eyebrows - On The Lash, Florida Mall
Teeth colour - Ronseal, Oak range from Poundland

Lottie and I made a pact at the start of the holiday that we'd keep the room tidy as we go, put away our clean and dirty clothes and definitely don't leave any food out. This was based on the previous Orlando holidays with the other two members of The Fam - while we discussed and made said pact, we 100%, wholeheartedly, categorically blamed Wifey and Sam for causing all the mess.

It turns out, it wasn't them at all. It was us.

The pact lasted 2 days. By day 3 the mess was slowly taking shape and now, by day 6, the room looked like a squat.

There's stuff everywhere – it's like we're unknowingly sharing the room with a big, feral family. You know, the scruffy looking ones all dressed in track suits and parkas that you see going shopping together at B & M on a Sunday morning, then pop next door to Pets at Home cos it's cheaper than taking the kids to the zoo?

"Ar God told ya, Britnaaaaay, yow ay avin a God guinea pig cos your granny's got asthma. Wait til she's jed"

There's food on the sideboard, crumpled up park maps, abandoned undies and an ever-growing pile of footwear that's taking on the appearance of an overflowing shoe recycle bin.

And the biggest pile of loose change you have ever seen in your life.

Where does all this change come from? Every time I come back to the room I'm weighed down with pockets full of tiny metal that I have to tip out on to the side. Then every time I go back out I can't be bothered to load myself back up for fear of ripping holes in my pockets. I'd thought about getting a bum bag, but I'm worried it'll cut in to my belly or just get lost in a fold.

And it's bad enough having these dollar bills made from the same paper as bog roll and everything that you buy having a hidden tax. I've not bought a single thing here yet that is rounded up to an exact dollar - anything and everything you buy totals to an amount with 4 decimal places, comes with a return of a handful of dog-eared, papier mache quality notes and minute coins that resemble a small amount of 3 mm washers being poured into your hands.

Oooh, speaking of undies I don't think I packed enough. I did a bit of "tidying up" which ended up with chucking all my pants into one drawer. Unfortunately, in the scruffy mixed up pants drawer the previously worn ones are hiding in between the clean ones and the only way I can tell if they're good to go is by giving them a sniff and then chucking them against the wall - if they stick, they're dirty.

One pair slid slowly down so there's a day or two in them yet.

I decided that this was an unacceptable situation for a well-known but not terribly well-recognised author like me (still not been spotted) and I hated the thought that I if I did bump in to someone that knew me, I'd feel uncomfortable knowing I'd got dirty pants on. So, I decided to do some washing so popped down to the Convenient But Terribly Expensive marketplace shop to see if they had any washing powder.

I asked the assistant, Caitlin-Kaytlynne Destiny Aurora if they had any Ariel. I don't think she understood my Black Country accent as the next thing you know another assistant appeared, ironically called Daz.

I tried to explain but he didn't get it either so Daz called over the manager, Cody-Corey Tucker-Bob Junior but he told me to go see Orlando Walmart. I hadn't got time to meet anyone else as it's taken me ages to write all these names down, so instead went back up to room 3149 and just stood in the shower wearing three pairs of pants and washed them all with Hard Rock soap. (Word of warning - if you're going to do this yourself, make sure you rinse out all of the soap. I found out my mistake the hard way after leaving Dudley Do-Rights Rip Saw Falls, soaking wet and frothing at the gusset).

For today's shenanigans we're going to be driven 45 minutes away into the everglades to be strapped in to a fan powered boat, bitten by killer mosquitoes and chased by alligators.

Sounds fun doesn't it?

It wasn't.

To be honest, once you've "putt-putt-putt putted" at 2 miles an hour along some of Dudley's finest canals in a barge, any other boat ride just won't cut it. (All good Black Country folk will get that last joke)

We arrived at our destination after driving through "real" Florida – a collection of really beautiful, posh looking houses and then some smaller, less attractive, scruffy ones that looked eerily abandoned with corrugated tin roofs and abandoned cars and bits of boat on the lawn. They looked just like the kind of houses that would have a dark, dirty secret – maybe a satanic shed, a ritual slaughter room or a shrine dedicated to West Bromwich Albion.

I was a little unnerved as the guy driving the cab was wearing a blue and white striped t shirt so I readied myself in case he tried to drop us off by a shanty house in the middle of nowhere and I had to give him the old Black Country "one-two" – a swift kick in the bollocks and run off.

Fear not, as we reached our destination unkilled and went straight to look in the gift shop. It was fab – everything on sale was alligator related, from alligator jewellery to alligator jam. Forever generous, I bought an alligator back scratcher for Wifey and some Smokey Chipotle Alligator BBQ sauce for Sam which I thought were great presents (post script – they weren't)

It was nearly our time to get on board for our wild adventure, so we went and waited on a spooky wooden pontoon with a load of other families ready to be sacrificed. Luckily, we were on a boat with a few young kids and fatties, so I fancied my chances of escape if / when the boat tips over.

Once safely on board and strapped in tight on a funny looking boat being steered by Captain Troy-Hickory III, we slowly glided out onto the lake and as soon as we were clear of the shoreline he opened up the big air con fan and we flew at warp speed along the marshes, searching for the elusive Florida alligator.

We bumped violently along the lake, holding on to our hats, having our chops wobbled about and being blasted in the face by loose bits of swamp weed and mosquitoes, all whilst not being able to hear a thing cos of the sound of the gigantic fan.

Am I selling it to you?

In 30 minutes of "searching" the lake for a scary reptile, Captain Troy-Hickory "found" one... albeit a very stationary one next to what he called a "nest" that looked to me like a floating pontoon tied down by an anchor. As he got closer and asked us not to stare at it too much, he slipped with the wheel and the boat hull bumped into the head of said "alligator". Despite a loud, tinny thud it never moved, arousing my suspicion further and reminding me instantly of the Monty Python parrot sketch.

"Best not look her in the eyes, folks, she's a feisty wun an could git nasty...", he said, convincing no-one as the alligator started to lilt to one side and slowly sink.

I don't think Cap'n Troy understood my question when I jokingly asked if it was a Norwegian Blue alligator. Although he did look at me funny all the way back and moved me right to the front of the boat "for ballast" as we went through extra choppy water.

Unsurprisingly we didn't see any more plastic alligators but we did see a few weird birds and a cow drinking at the water's edge, which is exactly what you'd expect for your $50 each and an $80 round trip taxi fare.

I could have saved all that cash for 4 gin and tonics at Hard Rock and waited til I got home - I can literally see cows out of my bedroom window!

Safely back on dry land despite the Cap'n Troy strangely bumping the boat against the pontoon just as I got off, my beautiful little snapper and I had a hot stroll around the Wild Florida zoo. We walked through stagnant swamps, held our noses around big piles of animal dung and gawped at sad, tatty looking creatures with no hope in their eyes. A bit like a walk down West Bromwich High Street.

Inevitably, we also came across some more plastic alligators (well, they never move do they? Isn't anyone else suspicious?) including 2 dead stiff "albino" ones that look like they've been painted with magnolia emulsion.

To be fair, they did have some ones that moved around a bit in a dirty great swamp, but I reckon these were remote-controlled by the keepers hiding in a secret hut. The gators only get twitchy when you pay $5.00 for a pouch of "alligator food" - which I guess is just enough to cover the cost of the remote batteries.

Time was ticking on as I'd booked something for Lottie, so we stopped for a quick lunch (I ordered the alligator burger and told her to make it snappy) and as soon as we'd finished headed to the other side of the smelly zoo.

I'd paid $39.00 (plus tax, making it just $43.6764456) for Lottie to have the "Swim with Sloths" experience. This turned out to be an underwhelming 15 minutes as she lined up with another 10 gullible tourists in a cage and when it was her turn, lightly patted the ugliest looking animal on earth while it messily ate corn on the cob upside down showing off its genitals.

I've said it before and I'll say it again - I could arrange all of this and more in Dudley. I could strap a fan off an old Ford Cortina to the back of a barge and for a tenner a pop show gullible tourists where the ducks nest between the shopping trollies on the canal. And we've got our own zoo with weird, smelly animals and even weirder, smellier zoo keepers.

Plus, if you want to see the *original* three toed sloths, just hang around the Wetherspoons in West Bromwich on benefits day. It's right next door to Greggs so if you wait long enough, you'll see them covered in food with their genitals out too.

We packed up our alligator gear and headed off to the waiting cab, where both of us power napped on the way back. Then, both of us woke the other up by sticking an alligator back scratcher up their nose. Top stuff.

When we returned to the hotel room, a note had been pushed under the door with my name on it (I'm Michael Hadley, so I knew it was for me).

At first I thought it was a reply to my Disgruntled of Dudley letter to Mr Hard Rock about the shocking lack of Barry Manilow memorabilia in his loud hotel, and if he wanted to take me up on my offer to donate my " *Barry - Live at Blenheim Palace*!" t-shirt for one of his glass cases.

Alas, it wasn't. It was something far better.

I'd been blogging these daft stories on Facebook each day as I went along, and I'd had a good reaction from lots of lovely folk along the way (most of them only interested in Lottie...pah) Two lovely people, Lewis Smith and Lisa Lynn from Blackpool had actually contacted the Hard Rock hotel directly and asked them to shove the note under my door, thanking me for the entertainment. How nice is that? To say I was touched is the understatement of the year. Thank you so much - it meant a lot to me and I was, and still am, genuinely humbled by your kindness.

Talking of lovely people, later that evening Lottie and I met up with a load of like-minded Brits at Margaritaville in Disney Springs for a little get together arranged jointly through two wonderful Facebook sites called Orlando Info Zone and It's Orlando Time.

What a lovely evening it turned out to be. Even my grumpy alter ego can't find anything remotely sarcastic to say here - everyone I met was delightful and all have the same shared interest of having a great family holiday in a magical place and making memories that will last forever.

Lottie was an absolute delight. She looked stunning and as we walked over to meet folk, I could not have been more proud to say she was my daughter. She chatted away to anyone and everyone, making polite conversation with people much older than her and being "big sister" to all the little kids. I'm truly blessed to have such a wonderful daughter and she means the absolute world to me.

The meet up was a roaring success and everyone had a great time. We laughed at funny stories, drank expensive cocktails and made new friends, all played out on a pontoon bar overlooking the lake as the Florida sun fell from the sky and a guitarist sang hits from Billy Joel. It was a wonderful evening.

We chatted and drank into the early hours and I left knowing that I've made some dear friends. I don't want to get too soppy but writing the daft blogs and the books has been incredible for me.

Life changing, in fact.

And so to bed to prepare for tomorrow's assault on Mr Disney's Secret Lair - The Magic Kingdom. I already know tomorrow is going to be an emotional day for me as the blogs and book all stemmed from last years trip to Disney and to The Magic Kingdom in particular. It truly is a wonderful place and the fact that I'm sharing the day with my precious daughter only makes it more special.

Let me tell you more of why being with Lottie is just *so* special...

I got a message from the girl in the office. I was a bit annoyed as we were in the middle of a stock take and I'd clearly told her not to disturb me.

"Your mum's just called. She said Lottie's in an ambulance…".

I dropped everything and ran to my car. Shaking like a leaf and overcome with fear, I drove like an absolute idiot through rush hour traffic, cutting people up and riding along pavements. In minutes I was near to the hospital but stuck behind a long queue of cars.

Then from behind me I heard sirens. I didn't know at the time, but it was the ambulance my Lottie was in.

As the ambulance sped past I seized the opportunity. I switched on my hazards, swung the car out in to the traffic and followed it, blaring my horn as loud as I could to warn the other cars to get out of my way.

I dumped my car somewhere near A & E and ran over to the entrance and in the distance I could just see the ambulance door open. I still didn't know it was my Lottie – all I saw was a big hunky paramedic step out of the back with a bundle of blankets in his arms and rush through the door.

It was only when I saw my wife appear from the same ambulance moments later that I realised.

She was still in her pyjamas. She still had her slippers on. She was ashen, shaking, staring in to a middle distance and had to be helped down and out of the ambulance by another paramedic.

She didn't see me as she was guided in to the hospital, but before I could get closer I was met by my dad.

My dad is not known for his affection. He's never been the kind of dad to show his feelings to me and my sister, or for the grandkids. I was both shocked and even more worried that the situation was that bad that he was there. But he was there at the very beginning of this, right when I needed him most. I'll never forget that.

He asked after Lottie, genuine concern on his face and in his voice. I said I didn't know as we both ran inside.

I saw Catherine. She crumpled in to a heap, sobbing, saying Lottie's name over and over again.

The two of us just held each other, crying, surrounded by folks with an assortment of injuries and ailments, none of them taking any notice. It was surreal – just a few hours before we were a normal family, all fast asleep in bed and ready for another day. And now I'm holding on to my wife in a sterile, cold hospital accident and emergency centre, trying to console her and tell her everything was going to be ok, that we're not going to lose our daughter.

My dad went for information and a few moments later we were all ushered in to an emergency suite where Lottie had been taken.

What I saw in front of me and what happened in the next few hours will never leave me.

My baby. My Lottie. Alone on a hospital bed with tubes in her mouth and up her nose, drips in her arm and monitors on her heart.

Totally lifeless. Limp. Arms flopped to the side and her head down on her shoulder.

Her skin was mottled and she was a bluey grey colour, like she'd been left out in the cold.

The doctor in charge had already ran blood tests and as he came and went from the room, nurses carried on doing things and talking in a medical language that we didn't understand.

We were ushered to one side, away from Lottie's bed and we managed to grab the doctor to ask him what was going on. It was becoming like a stereotypical scene in a film – worried relatives badgering the doc to find out the worst.

He told us they didn't know just yet and asked for us to be patient. He said they were doing all they can, and we'd know soon enough.

We sat in dumb silence as all around us was the chaos you'd expect in a busy A & E department – kids crying, adults wailing and medical staff running around.

Then there seemed to be a heightened level of tension. The machine next to Lottie's bed was beep-beeping away a little faster and all of a sudden two different nurses appeared. Then another, and another.

Then the doctor, accompanied this time by another couple of guys. He took charge of the situation as the staff gathered around Lottie's bed, silently and calmly going about his work as the nurses changed drips, passed instructions and pumped more antibiotics in to her little body.

Lottie was skin and bones. Just a tiny dot, surrounded by around 10 grown human beings who were trying to save her life.

We didn't know this for a few hours later, but at precisely that moment Lottie had started to quickly fade away.

She was going. She was leaving us.

In the melee of medical staff and instructions, we heard a phrase that didn't mean anything at the time but now strikes fear in to my soul – peripheral shutdown.

I've since learned that peripheral shutdown is a sign of impending death. To protect the internal organs, the body has an in-built safety mechanism that starves parts of the body of blood and oxygen. In turn, these parts of the body can suffer sudden and irreparable damage and even if you survive, the consequences remain.

The noise and general panic started to rise in the room as the staff frantically tried to keep Lottie alive, only pierced when a nurse had to use a massive needle to puncture a hole in to her little shin bone, directly in to the bone marrow so she could get a massive boost of life-saving fluids.

The crack of the needle in to and through her bone, followed by the shriek that Lottie made was horrific. The worst noise I will ever hear.

We were helpless. We stood and watched, completely numb and completely useless.

Whatever they did to Lottie, it would either work or she'd die. There was nothing else to do so the panic died down. We tried to get an update but one by one the staff disappeared, called away to perform miracles elsewhere.

The doctor caught up with us, and he politely told us to leave as Lottie was being taken away to a specialist ward so she could be monitored properly, and we should go and wait elsewhere and rest.

He also told us that Lottie had contracted strepticocal b menigitis. And that she may not survive.

To be continued.

Day 7 – Fun at the Magic Kingdom

Today's look: ***Disney Go-getter***

Cap - Free gift with a glue gun from Wickes
Vest – Pink, from George at Asda
Shorts – Pastel blue Primark, Brierley Hill

I awoke with a thicker than usual head this morning as a result of last night's meet up so today's blog is bought to you courtesy of the American paracetamol purchased from this morning's wobble to the Convenient But Terribly Expensive marketplace shop downstairs.

Braving the freezing blast of the aircon in just my Primark shorts and Asda vest top, I grabbed some coffee and donuts and approached the counter to try to get something to stop the clanging in my head. The girl behind till number one, Jaylee-Jolee Tiphanee La Bronx, had recommended a brand called ***ThrobGo*** and like all US drugs it came with its own bible-long disclaimer *.

* Copied here in part for the giggles.

"May cause heartburn, flatulence, excessive snot, anxiety issues, paranoia, ear wax, a mid-life crisis, piles, who said paranoia?, warts, eczema, ulcers, and **TELL ME WHAT WERE THEY SAYING ABOUT ME?**".

I noticed that the girl behind till number two, Grayce-Granola Maddison was selling a similar product called ***ThrobStay***, a product obviously aimed at men of my, ahem, age. I've no problem with men using erectile dysfunction pills – whatever keeps your pecker up. I used 'em once – not for my sex life but to stop me rolling out of bed.

I declined Grayce-Granola's offer of a free sample as I had to go upstairs and get my chubby bum into gear - me and Lottie had an appointment with the Big M himself at the Magic Kingdom.

Apologies in advance for a tiny bit of self-indulgence here but I know today is going to be an emotional day, and not just because I'm here with Lottie.

Today's visit to The Magic Kingdom comes almost exactly 12 months to the day that I posted my first daft blog on It's Orlando Time. That one blog has changed my life. I'd never blogged before and it's a fair to say that I never, ever expected what would happen as a result of it. The book that came from the blogs, the money raised for charity, the friends I've made, the opportunities I've been given and the life changing events that have unfolded since are all because of The Fam's visit to Orlando, and in particular the Magic Kingdom.

For those of you who liked and followed my stuff or bought a book, from the bottom of my heart I cannot thank you enough.

Anyway, enough of that sentimental nonsense, I've got a story to tell...

ThrobGo did the trick and with a clear head and perfectly coiffured hair, off we popped to Mr Disney's Secret Lair.

Lottie's dead good at planning. She has the folders and different coloured pens and everything. She had strategically planned all three of the Disney Smug Passes at convenient intervals in the day, so as soon as we got there we hit the ground running with Thunder Mountain.

After being chucked about on the good 'ol rickety train, we had a nice stroll across the park in the 100 degree heat to Tomorrowland, just in time for a drink in the shade as my skin was beginning to peel off. We had a poke around and watched loads of character meet n greets, then sat on a wall for a while and talked about how Lottie used to love meeting the characters and getting their autographs. That made me sad like Eeyore for a few minutes but I quickly had to shake it off as we had an appointment with Zurg and some aliens to zap.

Once we'd finished the Buzz Lightyear ride, I beat Lottie, much to her disgust, we headed back to Frontierland and one of my all-time favourite rides, Splash Mountain. I've no idea why this is the case – it's definitely not the best ride and it's really dated but I just love going on it. It could be because it lasts for ages so it feels like I'm getting my money's worth.

We dried off over lunch and as we had used up our Smug Passes, we were able to grab some more. We disagreed on the next ride - Lottie fancied doing Space Mountain and I really didn't. I'm usually ok on roller coasters, but there is just something about those in the dark that I don't trust. I always think there's going to be a loose girder, or something that's hanging off a beam that's gonna whack me on the head in the pitch black. Or decapitate the person next to me, so when we arrive back at the unloading bay I'm going to be sat next to a headless holiday maker.

It'd make the ride photo more interesting though.

Lottie managed to Smug Pass it so while she zoomed around Space Mountain I stayed put in Frontierland. I didn't feel great and as a result of the refried beans and corn on the cob I'd scoffed in Peco Bills Rootin Tootin Smokehouse Saloon, so I went to the little cowboy's room and made a Splash Mountain of my own.

As I waited for Lottie's return, I sat alone for a while and watched the park pass me by. I like doing this – it slows you down a bit in the middle of the chaos and makes you appreciate your surroundings instead of rushing from one ride or show to the next. And it provides lots of material to moan about.

My god, aren't Disney kids noisy?

It's only been a year since my last visit, but Mr Disney has evidently added a new show somewhere that teaches kids to scream at previously unrecorded decibel levels. They must hand out free Smug Passes to any kid that manages to shriek louder than a 747 and free entry all year to any brat that can scream loud enough to make Big Ear's ears bleed (wrong park character, I know but you get the drift).

During the same show, frustrated parents must have learned a whole new level of ambivalence by taking absolutely naff all notice.

By the time Lottie returned, I felt refreshed and ready to move on, determined to eek out as much of the day as possible. We went on Pirates of the Carribean, watched a devilishly handsome man tell awful jokes and make kids laugh pretending to be Capn' Jack Sparrow, giggled at the Monsters Inc Comedy Floor and I successfully tortured Lottie with It's A Small World.

I mentioned in the last book how Mr Disney had kept up with the changing economic and political times by splitting the UK away from Europe and putting up a wall around Mexico. I was happy to see he'd carried on with his work and introduced new "migrant" boats – every other boat on the ride is made up of North African refugees and at some point on the ride around the world they jump off and seek asylum.

Germany was swamped with them.

It's good to see North Korea back too, with a life size and spookily accurate doll of Kim Yung Un looking across a huge arsenal of weapons, all pointed at the US.

Not forgetting the good old U S of A, Mr Disney has made some changes here too. It's lost its place as the centrepiece of the ride and instead has drifted off alone, isolated from all the other previously friendly countries and heading for the dark ages. All the little male dolls have been replaced by Donald Trump lookalikes and all the female ones look like Ivanka. Weird...

Back in the park and my god it was hot and busy. Hotter than Satan's crotch and busier than the West Bromwich BetFred on giro day, you couldn't possibly walk in a straight line without bumping into someone, especially one of them big American families with colour coded t-shirts.

This segways nicely in to a new subject to moan about a bit more - directionally challenged people.

As previously mentioned in the Hollywood Studios chapter, it seems there's a growing phenomenon where stupid people just have no clue where they are going and are oblivious to the world around them. I've researched * this for your benefit dear reader and I present to you *Grumpy's Guide to The Directionally Challenged*.

* I haven't really.

The Stopper - identified by a sudden and dramatic stop directly in front of you as though they've just realised they've left the cooker on back home. Never an explanation and starts back off again as though nothing has happened. Potential damage from The Stopper includes spilt drinks, splattered food and chipped teeth.

The Wanderer - possessing non-directional legs that have no obvious connection to their brain, The Wanderer drifts effortlessly and aimlessly across the flow of the crowd causing multiple casualties. Often distracted by a map, a pretty bird or just simply the desire to walk on another piece of pavement for no apparent reason, The Wanderer causes more frustration than actual physical damage.

The Candy Crusher - usually bored mums who have been granted a "bit of me time" as dad pushes the monster truck stroller, The Candy Crusher gorms out in the crowd and goes at her own dreamy pace, transfixed by a brain rotting game where you splat fruit and continually aspire to be at a higher level than your imaginary friends. Eventually shouted back in to theme park reality by her grumpy husband for becoming The Wanderer and quickly shoves the phone back into her sweaty bra.

The Angry Map Reader - categorised by yells of "**I'm <u>LOOKING</u>!!!**" or "**Where's the castle**?" or "**It doesn't say on here what time the three o clock parade is, Kev**" The Angry Map Reader combines frustration, stupidity and ignorance by trying to read, think, walk and talk at the same time whilst holding a map in front of their face in the middle of a busy crowd, most of whom already know where they are going. Can cause multiple damage, mainly to themselves by walking in to a Disney lamp post or tripping up a gutter.

The Criss Crosser – a combination discipline. Part Wanderer, part Stopper, the Criss Crosser decides to walk *diagonally* across the flow of people, only to suddenly decide that they really wanted to be where they started and make a swift about turn and head back or across the flow. The Criss Crosser is a total idiot to be avoided at all costs.

The Big Family – a new one on me this year. Characterised by block colour t-shirts with their name on the back and the family name on the front, like "The Schumer's do Disney 2018" or "Jackson's On Vacation". This is where an entire family decide to go on holiday en masse, all walking together and all being simultaneously annoying, especially on rides where they insist on blocking the entire thing by sitting together.

The Ankle Nipper - everyone's favourite! This category includes folks with scooters, caravan sized strollers and those mini trailers that look like a kiddies wooden truck on wheels packed with food and cooking utensils, popular with South American families. Invisible in a crowd, The Ankle Nipper is the cause of many rows and damage to lower limbs, and is right up there at the top of the list of the most annoying folk in the parks.

And finally...

The Military Mum – complete with the laminated, colour coded daily planner and a detailed spreadsheet on her tablet as back up, The Military Mum marches purposefully from one pre-arranged, forcefully enjoyed experience to another. Don't mess with this one... reservations were made for Be Our Guest, meet and greets arranged and Smug Passes booked to a NASA degree of chronological precision MONTHS ago. Usually sporting full hiking gear, The Military Mum takes no prisoners in her quest to make sure everyone has a good time and woe betide any living thing that gets in her way. She gains extra strength and power from silently seething about her next to useless grumpy husband who's done naff all (as usual).

So there you have it, hope my pretend research has helped you.

Despite the crowds, the noise, the kids, the temperature, the queues, the cost, the blistered feet, the traffic jams, feeling sick after eating too much and the fact that I'll never be as good looking as Capn' Jack, we had a fabulous time.

We hit the wall before the fireworks so decided to beat the rush and decided to head home just as the sun was going down. Realising that this would be our last time here for a while, perhaps ever, I did get quite emotional.

And for once, so did Lottie.

We went upstairs to the large veranda that's part of the fabulous railway station, a secret hideaway that affords amazing views directly down Main Street and out toward the Magic Castle. We took some photos and had a longer than usual cuddle, before packing our gear up and heading out towards the Disney buses, desperately trying to dodge The Ankle Nippers, The Criss Crossers and The Military Mum's on the way out.

Day 8 - "I've paid for a 14 day Universal pass so let's make sure we get our money's worth on the last day, Day"

Today's look: *All Action Athlete*

Shorts - Sports Direct. Short, silky ones with side vents as worn by Kenyan marathon runners
Vest - Wolverhampton Indoor Market. Loosely fitted, teasingly showing one moob nipple
Headband - Used Dudley. Bought off a guy who claims it belonged to John McEnroe but I don't think he was being serious.

Today's look is deliberately "athletic" as this is our last full day and we planned to really go for it to make sure we get around all the bits of Universal we've missed. Like all wonderful folk from The Black Country, I do like to wring out every drop of value from each dollar that I've handed over to Mr Universal, so my challenge today was to walk round both parks and not miss a single ride, shop or toilet.

Getting about a bit also exposes me to more folk, especially in these shorts, and increases my chances of being spotted, thus winning my bet with Lottie. After 7 non-celebrity days here so far, I've accepted that this is unlikely to happen. Desperately looking for an alternative reason other than just people don't give a toss, I reckon my chances would have been better walking around with a face mask of the Grumpy Dad caricature instead.

Cos that wouldn't be creepy at all, would it?

So, onto today's adventure and our plans to go on every ride, especially the ones where you get a chance to get to experience how it must feel to be that one lonely sock in the tumble dryer. I do like roller coasters but they don't half mess me hair up. I want my coiffed barnet to look at its superb best for today's shenanigans, so in readiness I popped down to the Convenient But Terribly Expensive marketplace shop to get some gel or other product that would make it look frozen to my head.

The girl behind the till today, Rosetta-Alapecia, wasn't sure if they sold strong gel so shouted across to her colleague Janelle-Aurora Krystal-Chandalier and asked:

"Hey girl, you got anything that can keep this old guy rock hard?"

Janelle- Aurora smiled seductively but I politely declined her offer of another free sample of *ThrobStay* and returned to my room, hoping I'd have enough Elnett Maxi Hold to keep my bouffant in place after 2 goes on Rip Ride Rockit.

Once safely in the park, Lottie and I maxed out our Smug Passes in the first couple of hours, managing to get on quite a few rides. We both giggled like little kids at Minions, I had my hair messed up so it looked like a burst mattress on Rip Ride Rockit, we were both underwhelmed by The Mummy and both felt sick when we came out of Transformers after being violently chucked from side to side in an attempt to outrun a gang of angry zombies made out of bean cans.

All this expensively made excitement led us to lunch time so after a little browse in the shops, Lottie and I found a bench in the shade in pretend New York and for half an hour we sat and chatted away, eating a pepperoni pretzel with cheese sauce. Then we were serenaded by a fake Marilyn Monroe who reminded me a bit of my darling Holly Willoughby as we ate our ice cream. I'm still watching my waistline so chose the regular sized Ben and Jerry's Oreo and peanut butter milkshake at just 1250 calories a suck.

Looking back now, these little moments with Lottie were the best parts of the holiday. Just the two of us sitting in the sunshine, people watching and chatting away about daft stuff. At the time I didn't realise it as there is always so much going on, but it dawned on me since that this is the longest I've ever spent on my own with my little girl since she was poorly and I slept on the floor in the hospital ward while she was fighting for her life in an incubator.

I'm pretty angry with myself about that. She's 18 now and all grown up, and this is the most time in almost 18 years that we've done this. I'd like to think I've been a good dad to Sam and Lottie as both of them have grown up – I've loved them, provided for them and given them a good start in life. But I do feel totally ashamed of myself that I allowed work to come between me and my family and missed out on such a lot of them growing up.

Apprentice Grumpy Dad's take note.

We had prime New York pavement seats for The Blues Brothers show and having just missed it a couple of times this week, I was determined to shake a tail feather today. I love the movie and the two guys playing Jake and Elwood here both look, sing and dance just like the real thing.

I did my best clicky finger dad dancing, singing at the top of my voice and happily forgetting the fact that I'm a 50-year-old man dressed in cheap running gear. Lottie shuffled further away in embarrassment with each of my perfectly timed twists and was almost out of the park when I started to recruit other crowd members for a conga.

These guys were ace and I was dead impressed with the cool old dude on the sax - well dressed with a great soul voice he really got the crowd moving as he danced and played at the same time.

When he hits that high note, I bet you wouldn't get a credit card between the crack of his arse.

We headed over to The Simpsons bit and after a refreshing but ridiculously expensive Duff Beer and a Smug Pass go on the very funny Simpsons ride, decided to head back over to the other park to finish off our day. Despite Southern Rail's wildcat strike action at Harry Potter's pretend Kings Cross we were back over in Potterland in no time, managing to avoid The Stoppers, The Wanderers, The Criss Crossers and The Military Mums.

I mentioned bras in the description of The Candy Crushing Mum in the last chapter and while I'm feeling brave cos it's getting to the end of the book, I have a question for all you yummy Orlando ladies.

Since when did bras double up as mobile phone holsters?

Are they now being made with an extra pouch, or are you just podging 'em in?

This new phenomenon, along with nearly everything about women to be honest, completely bamboozles me.

Like most dopey eyed, one-track-minded male idiots, I love bras. I absolutely love 'em. They have always been of immense interest to me and I only have to see a flash of a flimsy, lacey strap to go as googly eyed and as weak at the knees as I did the first time I ever saw one in my mum's Grattan catalogue.

But aren't they meant to hold in and support beautiful bosoms rather than be a secret hiding place for your phone?

And, aren't you ever worried that when you reach in to get your phone that you could accidentally scoop out a floppy knocker?

Over in Orlando when it's horribly, sticky hot every day, it seems to me that the extra sweat could create the perfect environment for that to happen (if there's a scientist reading this and you need help doing some field research, I'm your man).

A friend of mine told me that she was out shopping once in the big Tesco in Dudley and was happily chatting away on the phone.

As most women do, she got carried away with the conversation and suddenly realising the time, hastily ended the call in the deep freeze aisle and quickly poked the phone in to her bra. Unbeknownst to her, she'd forgotten to lock the screen and a combination of reaching into the back of the deep freeze for mixed veg and a big erect nipple had accidentally purchased a set of rattan furniture, a pack of dog chews and a year's subscription to Amazon Prime.

Back to the story and we soaked up the last bit of sunshine in Harry Potter's Wobbly Shop Street and as the sky was starting to look a bit menacing, we decided to quickly make it over to Jurassic Park next door. Mr Universal has made so much money that he has special radars in his secret control centre and he can detect bad weather 15 minutes before it's due over his empire. This gives him the chance to close all his outdoor rides down in case some poor numpty gets struck by lightning whilst strapped in to a boat looking for plastic dinosaurs.

In this case, me.

Just as we reached the Jurassic Park log flume ride, the board went up to say that it was temporarily shut due to bad weather, and at that exact moment Orlando did indeed decide that everyone was having way too much fun so it sent down some angry rain to ruin everyone's day.

As people hurriedly reached for $15.00 ponchos to make themselves look like a human boil-in-the-bag, the heavens opened for a huge dose of thundery wet misery and Lottie and I were forced to take cover inside the Smug Pass queue for Kong. I didn't mind as it was dry and as we'd been rushing around it was a chance for me to write up my notes so far on today.

Or so I thought. As soon as my phone came out I got a:

"Fuh God's sssakkke Dad-uh. Put your phone away-uh".

Lottie was getting fed up with me writing my blogs even as we were heading up the M6 on travel day and ever since then she's been forever berating me for being on my phone (oh, the irony) so I've taken to writing stuff when she's not looking or getting up early in the morning before she's awake.

She also totally lost interest in my blogs around day 3 after hearing me laugh at my own jokes and telling her how many likes I'd got. She just doesn't get it at all. In fact, she didn't read my blogs from last year and didn't even read my book, stating that she wouldn't get most of my jokes as they were all written about a time before she was born.

I can't argue with that to be honest.

Even when I think I've written something good and got hundreds of likes and positive comments, she remains totally unimpressed and resorts to taking the mickey.

"Dad, you're not even funny" and * adopts nerdy scientist voice and pokes imaginary glasses on *.

"Well, statistically, the figures prove that I'm popular as I've got 236 likes, 64 loves and 34 "Laugh Out Louds" in only the first 95 minutes. That's 3.5157894737 reactions every 60 seconds. Oooh, I do love the math".

I had a feeling she'd moan about it as she'd been well prepped by Wifey – I found out that they'd had a secret conversation before we left and Lottie had been primed and armed with all manner of tricks, insults and comments to make me behave.

So, being the smart arse that I am, in readiness for Lottie moaning about me tapping away on my phone I'd bought a small notepad to jot ideas down as we trekked around the parks. This backfired spectacularly as not only did I look like some weirdo, pervert detective, looking suspiciously around at people, giggling to myself then making notes, Lottie found yet another reason to take the mickey out of me.

"Oh he's here again, Inspector Blue's Clues. What you found funny this time, a dead lizard?".

So we queued in a damp, tired silence for 40 minutes until it was our turn to see the big monkey kill loads of dinosaurs again. I wonder what they must feed him?

Orlando must have been terribly angry that day as the rain became biblical and put a wet full stop to our last few hours in the park, so we bailed back to the hotel to dry off and get ready for our last meal at Bubba Gumps.

As we gorged on Coconut Shrimp and I got merry on a few American beers I got a bit soppy, really hoping I'd made my little girl happy in the last 8 days. I sat across from her, getting pie eyed and telling her I'd had a great time as she told me to shut up and stop being weird. Trying to snap out of my dopey state, we then played a game where we went over our holiday "best bits" – best day, best ride, funniest ride, best show, best meal... it was fab.

We were still _in_ Orlando but already reminiscing about the amazing time we'd had. I knew then that I'd done my job – I'd created memories with my little girl that would stay with both of us forever. You can't buy that folks.

I would have recorded my exact thoughts at the time but Lottie had stolen my phone and thrown my notepad in the bin.

Pfft.

P.S. – still didn't get spotted.

Day 9 - Time to go home day

Today's look - ***International Jet Setting Chaveller***

Joggers - Drop crotch specials, H & M
T-shirt - Barry Manilow *"Mandy"* tour 1986
Flight socks - Poundland, Brierley Hill

Well my friends
It's time to go
To pack our bags
And leave Or-lan-do

It's been great fun
We've had a ball
Thanks for reading
I love you all *

(* Technically not true. Although I do feel I've got to know my readers over the last year or so, please don't take that the wrong way and turn up at my house with flowers and chocolates or anything. Although if you do, a small bouquet of pink roses, a Kinder Bueno and a bottle of Yellowtail would be nice. Oh, and a pigs dick for the dog so she doesn't feel left out).

It didn't take long for Lottie and I to pack this morning so after chucking my clothes in to my case (75% of which I didn't wear and are destined to go straight back up the loft for when I've lost some weight) I left Lottie monging out in room 3149 and headed out to the pool where I tried to defy physics and logic by getting an all over suntan in the remaining 2 hours I've got left.

As previously mentioned, I'm from The Black Country and we like to get our "munneys wuth" for everything. In this case, sunshine which technically I've paid for.

Getting value for money also extends to petty pilfering, especially when it comes to the Convenient But Terribly Expensive Marketplace Shop where the fools let you help yourself to posh condiments like really posh peanut butter, Philadelphia cheese spread and organic honey.

When I get back, I'm going to flog all these *"Ken"* Salad Dressings I've nicked on eBay – I reckon I'll break even on the holiday.

We've had an action packed 8 days so far and although it's been hot and sunny, I'm still whiter than a milk bottle. After spending enough money to set up a small business, I can't go home without a suntan, can I? In order to make my chubby face look a little more healthy and a lot less pasty, I had an idea - I should get one of those reflective sunscreens!

Genius idea as I've always wanted to see what I look like with sunburnt nostrils.

I guessed they'd sell em in the shop, so I waddled over in just me bright yellow Speedos and matching bumbag and asked the nice lady behind the till, Sharntelle-Chlamydia, if they had any in stock. Turns out they didn't but she managed to persuade todays chef, Chesnee-Diesel Jaxon Junior, to fettle something out of some Bacofoil and an old catering tub of Ken's Mayonnaise.

Comfortably plonked by the pool in the sun, I fell asleep in an instant, listening to Barry Manilow with my home made sun screen wrapped around my neck like one of them plastic things used to stop dogs licking their bits after they've been "done".

I awoke from a bad dream about drowning in a vat of mayonnaise to realise that it had started to rain and my home made sunscreen had doubled up as a funnel. Effectively, I'd invented human neck guttering with the added and now obvious flaw that water laced with left over mayo slime was being swiftly being channelled all down my throat, neck and chest.

I packed up my stuff and dashed quickly back to the room for one last shower, and once I'd washed off the remnants of Hawaiian Tropic and greasy condiment sauce, I changed in to my chavelling clothes. Lottie is always super organised, so she was already to go. I always think it's a sad moment when you leave a hotel room after a good holiday and this was no exception. We've had a lot of fun in this room, from laughing at American TV, chuckling about some of the stuff we've been up to and just acting daft as a result of being chucked together. It's precious time and I've enjoyed it immensely.

Strange how you become attached to a hotel room isn't it? Room 3149 at the Hard Rock Hotel, Orlando will always hold a very special place in my heart. It was with a great deal of sadness that I said a teary goodbye to the bed, lobbed the "V's" at the coffee machine and took one last look around the room to make sure I'd nicked as much as I could before closing the heavy door behind me.

We chucked our cases in with the rock band lookalikes at the concierge and headed out for a 3000 calorie lunch by the swimming pool, topped off with another one of those beers with an orange in it called Blue Moon.

I don't really like the beer to be truthful - I just like the gimmick of having an orange in it. Like a lot of simple things that amuse my childish brain, it makes me smile when I see it. Inside my head, I have a little happy character like the one in Inside Out, and every time he sees the orange in a beer he jumps up and down, clapping in happy excitement.

It's the same reaction when I see a bra strap.

The only problem with this orangey beer is that the orange got wedged in the bottom of the glass, only to be released as I took my last big greedy gulp, causing a Blue Moon Tsunami to wash over my chops and all over my new pink top.

This is not a new phenomenon. There is barely a Poncey item of clothing in my wardrobe that doesn't have some sort of canteen medal. Something mysterious seems to happen in that last millisecond as the fork or spoon travels the last inch in to my eagerly opened mouth, causing the contents of the fork or spoon to topple, usually landing on my chin, chest or belly, leaving behind a splattered stain equivalent to a blob of paint.

I have no idea why this is – I don't have the shakes, I don't think I'm a messy eater and, as it stands at the moment, other than an inability to hold in a trump I have full control over my bodily functions.

I've come to accept that this is my lot and I'm just one of life's messy eaters - I could make an upside-down sloth look like he had the table manners of little Lord Fauntleroy.

With a full belly, a new orange stain on my top and $70.00 less in my pocket, Lottie and I had a last little look around the lobby and took a few final photographs before jumping in to our cab to be whisked over to Orlando Airport.

My flying anxiety kicks in as soon as I get a first sight of planes coming in to land or when I spot the air traffic control tower and today was no different. That's the trigger point for me to reach for my hidden bit of vodka apple juice and a couple milligrams of tranquilizers, just to take the edge off proceedings and give everything a warm, pastelly glow. It also starts to turn me in to a happier, dopier version of myself and makes me believe I'm MUCH funnier than I actually am.

Which is why, in the mile-long queue to clear airport security. I whipped out my Universal room key and laughingly asked the big US Immigration guy, Chuck-Eugene Cleetus Junior:

"Is this the Express Lane, mate?"

Chuck-Eugene had no sense of humour. He did, however, have a really big assistant who took a giant's step forward, politely placed his massive hand on my shoulder and quietly advise me to calm down and not breach security protocols. Spoilsports.

Once clear of security, we headed through duty free and an opportunity to load up on booze so I can enjoy the flight back. I'd paid in advance to use one of the posh lounges again, mainly cos it works out financially better due to the amount of vodka I can drink, but also so I can pilfer more food.

I'd come prepared with a fold up, zippable Mickey Mouse lunchbox I'd bought for a quid from Primark to avoid suspicion and while Lottie looked on in disgust, I hastily rolled up half a dozen pastrami, turkey and swiss cheese sandwiches behind my PC.

You see a laptop - I see a modesty screen perfectly sized to make a secret airplane picnic.

Lottie wandered off for a trawl around duty free whilst I sat alone, writing away and reflecting on a wonderful few days, broken only by frequent trips to the bar and more frequent trips to the little pilot's room. Forty-five minutes before take-off, Lottie came to collect me and delicately helped her drunken fool of a Dad to the boarding gate, on to the plane and out of Orlando.

*****

The flight itself, or what I can remember of it as I was as higher than a hippy in a hot air balloon, was boring and uneventful save for a few things.

I had the middle seat, which I hate, and had absolutely zero leg room - there's more free space and comfort on Rip Ride Rockit.

And the friendly guy sitting next to me was enormous. Like, gigantic.

In my soppy state, I always talk to strangers as I think I'm REALLY interesting and I always seem to make a fool of myself – as my new mate, the BFG next to me, witnessed on more than one occasion. First off, I managed to spill my drink on him, then I fell in to a dribbley sleep leaning on his big comfy shoulder and finally I dropped my rucksack on his head trying to find my headphones.

He and Lottie looked at each other across the seats with a knowing air of sympathy and in an instant I think he felt her suffering.

Also, the pretty Virgin stewardess serving us the food and drink had the most enormous boobs I'd ever seen in my life. They were humongous.

When I first saw her wander down the aisle I proper panicked, thinking something was wrong as she had already blown up her life jacket under her uniform.

Never mind hiding your phone in your bra - she could have got a whole call centre in there.

I didn't stare, honest.

An unfortunate side effect of too many stolen turkey and swiss cheese sarnies, mixed with fizzy gin and tonics at 30,000 feet, is flatulence. You can try as hard as you like – you can wiggle in your seat and clench your butt cheeks together to try and keep it trapped, but sometimes it's just better for you to make like Elsa and Let It Go.

Which I did. Quite a few times.

I did one fart so loud that the four people in front of me turned round and for a minute I thought I was on The Voice.

I slept, trumped and wrote an entire chapter about Lottie that when I read it back later made absolutely no sense at all. The flight seemed to drag on and was easily the worst part of the week so I won't waste any more of your time and just fast forward to our arrival at back at home in The Black Country.

Wifey and Handsome Son had hugs galore, Molly the Cockapoo got dead excited and piddled on my Poncey Ted Baker trainers and I had a proper cup of Yorkshire Tea. One of the side effects of the tranquilizers and booze is that I get the mad munchies and today it was a craving for toast.

Anything on toast. Sometimes just more toast.

I scoffed my toast as homecoming gifts were furtled out of our cases. I dunno why but Wifey was singularly unimpressed with her new genuine alligator claw back scratcher and Forrest Gump badges. In my opinion it's an improvement on the garment steamer I got her for Christmas 2016 (that was a Frozen Christmas, I'll tell ya)

I was filled in with the last eight days' worth of Fam shenanigans, which included new additions to the ever growing list of items that the dog is allergic to and if swallowed will cause a £500.00 vet's bill. I found out that my uncle's scaffold company had gone to the wall and my cousin's attempt to revive the kid's game "Genga" had collapsed.

Oh, and Dudley's oldest paperboy had died at 84. The bloke at 86 never did get his papers.

And that was that. Back to normality.

I felt a jet lag fuelled power nap coming on but before I had chance to close my eyes, Lottie disappeared to see her lovely boyfriend, meaning we were apart for the first time in 10 days.

As I watched her jump in to his arms and then speed off in his car, my heart ached.

I missed her straight away.

My eyes closed as I tried not to think about it and instead just concentrated on the amazing experience we've just had and the precious time and lifelong memories we've made. I hope that she will always remember this past ten day, and by committing it all to paper is a way to record the moments and ensure that it should never be forgotten.

Not that she'll ever read it mind. She thinks my stuff is utter drivel.

I did write something that Lottie has read though. Just recently, actually.

Wanna see? Come on then...

Later that day, we found ourselves sitting in silence in a small private room on the children's ward of Wordsley Hospital. Our baby girl was in front of us. She was in a small incubator with wires attached to her chest, drips in her veins and an oxygen tube up her nose.

She was still limp, grey and lifeless.

But breathing.

There was hope.

We had tried to pull ourselves together. We went home to quickly get changed and freshen up. Calls were made to work to tell them I'm not coming back for a while. Relatives were contacted and given the news - some were on the scene immediately while others offered help with little Sam or back up for real life like shopping and housework.

All sent love.

We were told of the meningitis infection Lottie had contracted and how they planned to treat it. They were going to intravenously pump Lottie full of strong antibiotics, and hope that they had caught the infection in time for her to survive and have no lasting damage to her health.

We couldn't do anything but wait. Wait to see if our world was about to be turned on it's head and we would lose our baby girl or wait to see if we were the kind of parents that were blessed with good fortune.

So that's what we did. Just sat and waited.

The children's ward was quite small, with only around 20 little ones in total. It was in an old annexe to the main hospital, reached by a myriad of alleyways and then up a clanky old lift. The whole hospital was ancient and rundown, cold and dark with an awful feeling of despair. It was suffering from a chronic lack of cash as the budget had been spent on a more modern hospital in Dudley, so the staff on the children's ward just had to make do with what they had.

Which they did with an amazing amount of love, care and attention for the kids and a dedication to their job that is truly humbling (If you are a doctor or nurse reading this, you have my utmost admiration and respect for the job that you do. You truly are the best of us). Although Lottie was in a private *room, we were never made to feel in the way and we were treated with the same attention that she had – always a kind word, a cup of tea and positive thoughts of support and encouragement that she would get better.*

A few children lost their battle to survive in the time we were there with Lottie. A few parents were heartbroken, enveloped in sadness and grief at the loss of their child. I cannot begin to comprehend how that must feel.

I slept there every night for the next two weeks. Sometimes on the floor, sometimes slumped in one of the big old uncomfortable armchairs. I couldn't leave my little girl on her own, couldn't bear the thought that she would be all alone in a cold dark room, crying or in pain.

She was so small. She had no idea what was going on in her world and no way of communicating to us how she felt. But that didn't matter – I wanted to be there to hear about the little bits of progress that she was making, desperate for good news each time a nurse came in to check on her. Secretly, I also wanted to be there in case something happened, and we weren't lucky. The image of an emergency where she started to fade or worse still leave us altogether without her mum or dad there filled me with dread.

It was during one of these long, lonely nights that I wrote my daughter a letter. Too small to comprehend what was happening to her, I wanted her to know what she'd been through when she was older.

If she got older.

The letter explained what had happened, where we were and how much she was loved and cherished by her mum and dad. I wanted to capture the moment so she would see and hear the raw emotion in my words and, if she survived, know how lucky we all were that she made it.

I also vowed that if she did survive, the letter would never be opened or read until she reached eighteen years old.

The letter was partly inspired by the lyrics of a song called "Yellow" by Coldplay and a few lines in particular. Although it was in the charts at that time, I didn't find out until much later that it was actually released on the day Lottie was born.

Your skin

Oh yeah your skin and bones

Turn into something beautiful

You know you know I love you so

You know I love you so

The song means more to me than anything else I've ever heard and captures everything about that time. The panic, the desperation, the fear, the total helplessness and the desire to do anything, anything at all to make Lottie better.

Your skin

Oh yeah your skin and bones

Turn into something beautiful

And you know

For you I'd bleed myself dry

For you I'd bleed myself dry

The letter was sealed in an envelope before she left hospital and hidden in a drawer under the bed.

*****

Nearly three weeks on from the early morning phone call, Catherine and I carried our baby girl together out to our car and drove her home. She has no major damage and made a full recovery, although in her teens she developed an aversion to her dad chewing.

Lottie opened the letter in front of me on her eighteenth birthday.

Happy Birthday Angel.

By the time you read this, your world will be entirely different to the one you find yourself ~~in~~ ~~the~~ ~~the~~ ~~moment~~. Hopefully, today you ~~are~~ will ~~be~~ be sharing your eighth birthday ~~together with~~ - Me, Mum Sam. ~~and you~~. I hope you have a day to remember, filled with nice surprises, presents and love from your friends and the rest of your family. and I hope you're enjoying life, and that all your ~~everything~~ ~~you~~ dreams ~~things~~ ~~is~~ are within ~~your~~ reach.

I want to tell you the story of how we nearly lost you, and I feel that if I write ~~it~~ it all down now, you'll realise how important you are to us, and how much we love you after everything we went through together. ~~We~~ ~~probably~~ ~~bad~~ ~~we you~~ ~~powing~~ ~~of~~. I'm sitting in a chair in a little room on the Children's ward at Wordsley Hospital. It's Sunday 22nd of July ~~2018~~! You are in a ~~to~~ small metal cot, with sensors attached to your hands and chest, connected to a machine that monitors your breathing, heart rate and oxygen. ~~Totally~~ ~~you forgotten~~. A small transparent box has been placed round your head, with a tube pouring oxygen in to help you breathe. Part of your hair (incredible, thick, spiky black hair - where did that come from?) has been shaved away just above your left ear and an intravenous drip has been inserted into your scalp. This feeds your fluid and nutrients as we can't give you any milk yet. (your favourite) You've been here since Thursday morning, and your mum and I have hardly left your ~~s~~, since then (I've been sleeping on the fldout next to your cot) All the doctors and nurses have been making a big fuss of you, and you've had the best attention and care possible.

Last Thursday was the worst day of my life. You were poorly in the night, and we couldn't work out what was wrong with you. We fed you, and loved you to sleep, and thought that you would be better in the morning. I went to work at seven o'clock, thinking that you would be fine. At nine o'clock you were in the Accident and Emergency ward at Russells Hall hospital, surrounded by doctors and nurses (eleven at one stage). I was there with your mum and your Grandad Donald. We were very scared. The more the doctors did to your little body the more we worried we would lose you. Even though you were only a few weeks old you were very strong and you screamed and yelled to let them all know you didn't like what they were doing. At one stage, you had a drip in both arms, your head, and when you started to deteriorate a tap was put directly into your bone marrow through your left shin bone. Not long after this we were told that this is the time that you started to die, and your body had had enough. The doctors knew this and did everything they could to bring you round. After about fifteen minutes you were pumped full of fluids and antibiotics, and the doctors had saved your life. They all slowly disappeared, and left me, your mum and grandad to look after you until you were moved to the children's ward. You were diagnosed as having meningitis and

You stayed in the hospital for just over two weeks making a good recovery (even managing to put on weight - you were 8 pounds when you went in, and nearly ten when you came out) It was very hard for everyone while you were in hospital. Sam was upset because he didn't understand why he had to live at his nannys house. your mum and I were upset because we hardly saw each other, and we were all upset because of what you had been through. all of this.

You were still a beautiful baby. Thick spikey black hair, big blue eyes and a lovely smile. I can't imagine two more beautiful children than you and your brother, and I'm humbled at the thought that I am your father.

~~You I need to ~~

who knows what may have happened in the last eighteen years? I know one thing is for certain - that as long as I am still alive, I will love you with all my heart, and as much today and every day as I did when you were first born. Never forget that Lottie, please never forget that.

I hope this letter doesn't upset you - that is not the intention. I want you to know that you must take every opportunity in life, make your own decisions and be who you want to be. Always listen to other people, and take advice when needed. But always always always be your own woman.

Love for ever

Dad.

"Your skin and bones
Turned into something beautiful
And do you know? I'd bleed myself dry?
For you I'd bleed myself dry"

Epiblog - Dudley calling

Today's look - *Jet Lagged Tramp*

Jeans - Bilston Sunday car boot sale
Shirt - Scruffy, buttons missing
Boots - Steel toe capped, scuffed, uncomfortable

Blimey, I've only been home 24 hours and I want to go back already. It's only the sudden and unexpected bouts of narcolepsy and a maxed-out credit card that's stopped me from firing up the laptop and persuading Wifey to go again for Christmas this year.

What a blast! Lottie and I only stayed 8 nights but I reckon we crammed a fortnight in. We skipped entire lazy pool days and just did the fun stuff, never missing an opportunity to go on a thrilling ride, to have a laugh together or meet up with some truly lovely people.

The Hard Rock hotel is a fabulously cool place (albeit with an appalling lack of recognition for Barry Manilow) and I have some fabulous memories of the lobby DJ, drinking too much by the pool bar, the Convenient But Terribly Expensive marketplace shop (especially my favourite, Sharron-Patty Fanny-Loulabelle Lorreeese) and precious moments in room 3149.

In the parks, we screamed from the adrenaline rush of the roller coasters, we were amazed from some of the 3D experiences, we laughed at the comedy stuff and cried at the shows (only me at Beauty and the Beast though).

But most of all we had fun. And that's what it's all about, having fun and making memories. It doesn't matter if it's your first or your twentieth time, your marriage proposal, anniversary or birthday, or massive family holiday, the whole idea is to enjoy yourself.

I **AM** a Grumpy Middle-Aged Dad. The persona comes with the age, the territory, and too many decades of slogging me guts out in Dudley. Too many tedious obstacles to overcome in my desire to scrap and fight for my share of a living in order to keep The Fam fed, watered, safe and happy.

But my trips to Orlando have definitely blunted my Grumpy edge, and after seeing first-hand the magical effect it has on families including my own, it makes you realise there really is more to life than work.

Grumpy Dads! Stop slouching, sit up and take note - those extra, unrecognised, unrewarded hours spent at work, those nights slumped over the laptop working at home and weekends working at trade shows all eat away in to your precious time with the kids.

Been there, done that, got the grumpy t-shirt. And the emotional and physical scars.

No amount of money or success can make up for that lost time and trust me, it's really, **REALLY** not worth it.

We really did have a great time. I annoyed her a lot, cos that's part of a dad's job, especially when it came to selfies ("God Dad will you stop taking pictures of me"), eating (Fuh, God's sake Dad why have you got to chew so loud?") and writing ("Dad, you're not even funny. Will you put that phone way?"). But throughout our time together we got on great and didn't have a single cross word.

It was made even more special by the fact she's just turned 18. If you have stuck with me all through the book, you will know she's lucky to have made 18 days, never mind 18 years, so this was an extra special birthday.

That's why I wanted to do this with Lottie now, before it's too late and before she's too old.

To show her one last time that she's my little girl now and forever.

To show her that she has a dad who loves her and wants nothing more than to make sure she has a great time.

To make memories that will never fade, not even when the inevitable happens and we will forever be apart.

My world is a much better place cos she's in it.

Thanks for reading.

(Not so) Grumps out.

Lottie's afterword

It's what you've all been waiting for...

It's finally my turn, so I present to you:

Lottie's (and Grumpy Middle-Aged Dad) Adventures in Orlando

aka

"How to control your toddler parent"

So yes, my dad is THE Grumpy Middle Aged Dad. But honestly, you have no idea what he's like in real life. You all know and love him as the funny chubby man who makes you all giggle at your phones when you should all be working but honestly, you have no idea what he's like in real life.

I swear it's like being on holiday with a needy overgrown child.

Frequent trips to the toilet, spilling food and drink all over himself, constantly wandering off and getting lost... not to mention the crying.

Who cries at The Little Mermaid?

And that phone... aaaaarrggghh

He was forever looking at it, especially when he'd just posted something on here and was obsessed with how many likes he got. He'd get all excited as soon as his phone pinged:

"Lot, Lot... look, 58 likes in 25 minutes. Not bad is it that, eh?"

"Look, Lot, Marjorie from Milton Keynes thinks I should do the Edinburgh fringe"

When he wasn't on his phone, he got this saft little notepad out. Oh my god, he looked like a right nutter. We'd be standing in a queue and out of his manbag (he called it a rucksack but trust me it's a manbag) he'd whip out this little notepad, look at someone and then start making notes about them. I'm amazed he didn't get punched.

I wouldn't mind so much but he robbed most of the jokes off me.

The American names - my idea

The names of the daft people that can't walk straight in parks - also my idea

And, he's always taking ridiculous selfies with me, knowing full well I do not want a selfie and then posting them thinking it's hilarious......IT'S NOT!

The worst is the chewing though. And eating in general. It's like he's got blunt teeth and everything that goes in his mouth has to be mashed up by his clanking jaw. And he can't even eat ice cream off a spoon right, he just washes his tongue round the other side of the spoon and dribbles ice cream down himself.

So yeah, when he wasn't snoring, chewing loudly, trumping, laughing at his own jokes, being obsessed with his phone, spilling stuff down him or drunk, we had a great time!

In truth, he is generous, for the most part funny, and he's fun to be around. Most people like him and I think it's amazing what he's done with the book (Dad you owe me 10 quid for that). I'm so grateful and lucky to say he's my dad and I'm so glad all you lovely people like him, it finally takes his friend count up to 6!

Afterword

Dear reader,

Well done for getting this far and thank you for coming on this journey with me – I am truly grateful.

The journey to completing this book has been very different to my first one. The original Grumpy book was my first attempt at becoming a literary genius and as a result was a bit clunky. Not surprising really as it was cobbled together on the run in Orlando, mashed about a bit in Dudley and finally glued together with lots of Chinese take aways and cheap Aldi booze in my kitchen.

Literally.

With this one, I tried to use a little more craft so it did justice to Lottie's story.

I carried Lottie's experience with me since she was just three weeks old and this book has been a great release to me – almost therapy if you will. I relived the story through the book and I'm not ashamed to say that I spent many hours blubbering into my gin as I replayed every horrific moment in my head.

The meningitis story is retold as accurately as my old brain will allow. Some details have got lost in the fog of time, but I vividly remember the feeling of total despair and helplessness as we watched our girl fade away, only to be pulled back from the edge. I remember lying on the floor next to her as she lay in the incubator, too scared to fall asleep in case she woke up and needed me. And as she recovered, I remember writing the letter.

The letter was sealed in an envelope and hidden away, where it remained for almost 18 years. It was given to Lottie on her birthday – there was just the two of us in a restaurant and we sat and cried together for hours. She had no idea how bad the situation was, or how close she'd been to death, so it had quite a dramatic effect on her. Reading the letter now and capturing the spirit of those moments, it's quite remarkable how the fighting spirit she showed us as a little baby as stuck with her throughout her young life.

But we were lucky – Lottie survived thanks to the amazing doctors and nurses at Russells Hall hospital in Dudley. My one regret is that I never got to thank them personally for that morning when they saved my daughter's life. The staff who work in our NHS are truly incredible and although they get the credit they deserve from the British public, the entire service is massively underfunded by government and the angels that perform miracles every day are hugely underpaid.

A little while after Lottie was given the all clear, Catherine and I went back to the hospital and donated a "portable" television with a built-in video player to the children's ward. The TV was massive and weighed an absolute ton – the only thing "portable" about it was the fact that it had a handle on the back to drag it along the floor. We did this as there was only one TV on the ward between all the kids and many of them would spend hours alone in bed when their parents couldn't visit.

Many parents in our position are not so lucky. I cannot being to imagine how that must feel.

The decision to donate the proceeds of this book to the Meningitis Now charity was an easy one. They carry out amazing work in the research and prevention of meningitis and offer support to children and families who have been affected by this terrible disease. Every penny they get goes toward preventing a situation like ours – trying to stop some poor mum and dad having to rush their child into hospital to be saved by the heroes and heroines of our NHS.

All of the money that you have paid for this book (except the bit that Mr Amazon takes) will be handed over to Meningitis Now and I will keep a running total on my Facebook page.

The fact that you have bought this book means that you are one the good guys, and your money will help. I really, truly hope that you have enjoyed it.

If you haven't bought this book, or if you've borrowed it from someone else, give your head a wobble and go off and make a donation.

Lottie and Michael Hadley,

Monday 6th of August 2018

Toy Story Land , Hollywood Studios

Printed by Amazon Italia Logistica S.r.l.
Torrazza Piemonte (TO), Italy

41341139R00075